To Sarah
Bringer of tea and insights

ANNE WINDSOR started her practice in 1993 in Salt Lake City, Utah. She received professional certification from the American Federation of Astrologers (PMAFA) in 1996 and now consults with clients, businesses, and students from around the world. She writes the popular weekly e-mail forecast column "Good Heavens™," available through her websites at www.annewindsor.com or www.astrologyforeveryone.com. She frequently lectures at national conferences and is well-known throughout the astrological community for promoting professional standards among astrological organizations and assisting other astrologers in building successful astrological careers.

MAPPING YOUR SOUL'S PURPOSE

Discover Your Karma & Destiny

Anne Windsor

Llewellyn Publications
Woodbury, MN

First Edition
First Printing, 2006

Book design by Donna Burch
Cover art © Photodisc
Cover design by Kevin R. Brown
Llewellyn is a registered trademark of Llewellyn Worldwide, Ltd.

Chart wheel was produced by the Kepler program by permission of Cosmic Patterns Software, Inc. (www.AstroSoftware.com)

Library of Congress Cataloging-in-Publication Data

Windsor, Anne.
    Mapping your soul's purpose : discover your karma & destiny / Anne Windsor.—1st ed.
        p.   cm. — (Astrology made easy series)
    Includes bibliographical references.
    ISBN-13: 978-0-7387-0673-3
    ISBN-10: 0-7387-0673-6
      1. Astrology and reincarnation. 2. Karma. I. Title. II. Series.

    BF1729.R37W56 2006
    33.5—dc21   2006045269

Llewellyn Worldwide does not participate in, endorse, or have any authority or responsibility concerning private business transactions between our authors and the public.
    All mail addressed to the authors is forwarded but the publisher cannot, unless specifically instructed by the authors, give out an address or phone number.
    Any Internet references contained in this work are current at publication time, but the publisher cannot guarantee that a specific location will continue to be maintained. Please refer to the publisher's website for links to authors' websites and other sources.

Llewellyn Publications
A Division of Llewellyn Worldwide, Ltd.
2143 Wooddale Drive, Dept. 0-7387-0673-6
Woodbury, MN 55125-2989, U.S.A.
www.llewellyn.com

Printed in the United States of America

Acknowledgments

Many thanks to the countless clients and students who graciously shared the most private details of their own personal paths. Without their trust and confidence in astrology, this book would never have come to fruition.

I am forever grateful to my son Adam for his unending confidence as the deadline loomed large on the calendar and to Annette Wright for making the office run smoothly whenever I had to write.

Thanks, too, to Stephanie Clement, Andrea Neff, and Kevin Brown at Llewellyn, all of whom helped tremendously in seeing this project through to completion.

Contents

Introduction
Soul Train: Where Are You Headed?

Folks have been looking for a sign ever since the first falling star arced across a midnight sky. In our world of microwave meals and sitcom sarcasm, it's easy to get caught up in the busy-ness of life. We race around and fill our space with the stuff of a supposedly successful life. It is only when we come to one of life's inevitable but confusing crossroads that our souls long for understanding and inspiration.

Fortunately, the delicate dance of the cosmos provides a bounty of cues and clues about who you are, who you've been, and where you're headed. In fact, your soul chose the exact moment in time when the pattern of the heavens would reveal the perfect road map for your journey. Just as with any map, you'll get further, faster if you take the time to understand the signs and symbols and at least figure out how to hold the darn thing.

Astrology is the ancient language of the stars, and like any new language, you'll run across a few tongue twisters and mindbenders. The good news is that you don't have to speak fluent "astrologese" to understand your soul's purpose. This book shows a simple way to read your own map and decipher your own soul's code.

As you explore each part of this book, the celestial schemes and themes in your own chart will quickly emerge. You'll receive confirmation of some of your deepest dreams as well as new insights into your past, present, and potential. Even if you discover that you've missed a few connections along the way, there's still time to change course and get back on track.

That's the real value of astrology. Go ahead. Spend some quality time studying your own map, get a lay of the land, and plan your itinerary. But the real fun begins when you take that first step, climb aboard the soul train, and go where your spirit guides you.

Astrology 101: What You Need to Know to Use This Book

Astrology is an incredibly versatile tool and can be used to predict the weather, time the opening of a business, understand your relationships, and everything in between. Thousands of books have been published, each highlighting astrology's unique capacity to define and describe any aspect of your life.

As you read through this book, you'll detect a distinctly spiritual emphasis. If you already know a thing or two about astrology, you'll notice right off the bat that some of the traditional components in a birth chart are not included in this book. Not to worry. *Mapping Your Soul's Purpose* simply focuses on the spiritual indicators hidden in your chart.

Hopefully, this book will excite and entice you to learn more about astrology, at which time you can master all those weird words that go flying by whenever a gaggle of astrologers gather. But for now, as you open the doorway into the secrets of your soul, here's the least you need to know about how to read your own map.

Planets

Planets reflect the many urges, impulses, and desires of your personality. Every chart has the same planets in it, but the unique combinations of sign and house placements make your chart, well, unique. Astrologers make use of glyphs so they don't have to write down the names of all those planets and signs over and over again. The notation for a planet includes a glyph for the planet as well as the sign it's in. So, instead of having to write "Mercury in Sagittarius," astrologers can say the same thing with a few simple strokes of the pen: ☿♐.

Most astrologers lump the Sun and Moon in with the planets, primarily because we'd rather talk about you and your chart rather than waste our breath saying "the Sun, Moon, and planets" over and over again. The important thing to remember is that the influences of the Sun and Moon are just as potent as any planet.

The following is a quick description of each planet's role in your soul purpose.

Planet	Glyph	Primary Impulse
Sun	☉	To create
Moon	☽	To respond, nurture
Mercury	☿	To learn, communicate
Venus	♀	To relate, acquire
Mars	♂	To act, fight
Jupiter	♃	To explore, expand
Saturn	♄	To be responsible
Uranus	♅	To break with tradition
Neptune	♆	To seek out the divine
Pluto	♇	To control your fate

Signs

Planets move through the heavens in pretty predictable orbits around the Sun, but from our view on Earth, it looks as though they're putting on a show just for us. Astronomers and astrologers of ancient times were absolutely convinced that our planet was the center of the cosmos and that every planetary player, including the Sun, revolved around our humble little planet Earth. Even though that theory was proven wrong hundreds of years ago, we're still stuck viewing the heavens from our Earth-centered, or geocentric, position.

In actual practice, astrology's capacity to provide helpful guidance and insight is not diminished at all by the fact that the Sun is center stage in our solar system. It's all about appearances and perception. In this case, it still appears that the planets are circling our own little corner of the cosmos. Thanks to the invisible zodiac belt that circles the Earth, we can still observe the planets rambling and roaming against the backdrop of the twelve signs of the zodiac.

What do we mean by "sign"? A sign is really just a set of characteristics concentrated into one single celestial slice of the sky. There are twelve signs that make up the zodiac. Originally, they lined up with the constellations of the same names, but now the signs are an equal and elegant division of the zodiac, each one a perfect one-twelfth division of the heavens.

The influence and impact of each sign has been defined and refined for thousands of years. When someone asks you "What's your sign?", the person is really inquiring about which part of the zodiac the Sun was lighting up at the blessed moment of your birth.

Each planet represents a particular part of your spirit. The sign each planet was traveling through on your birthday defines how it expresses itself in your quest for understanding. For example, if your Moon, which reflects your emotional nature, was visiting the reserved sign of Capricorn at the time of your birth, your own emotional expression is bound to be a bit cool and cautious, at least until you warm up to someone. Contrast that with someone born with the Moon in outgoing, over-the-top Sagittarius. It's the same Moon seeking out emotional awareness, but since it is influenced by a different sign, that person's experience of emotions will be markedly different.

Think of signs as adverbs or adjectives in the language of astrology. If the planet is the subject, the sign tells you how it does its thing. There's just one catch: every sign is a complex combination of lovely angel and little monster. Only you can keep your eye on the prize and integrate the higher vibration of that sign. Or, you can turn away from all of your good intentions and just start behaving badly. You may vacillate between the two extremes, especially when you're trying to navigate difficult times. Fortunately, the heavens are infinitely patient, and the positive side of any sign is up for grabs anytime we choose.

As with planets, astrology uses glyphs to represent the actual sign in astrological notation. This may sound complicated, but it really isn't. In fact, our brains have long been programmed to respond to pictures and symbols, signs and glyphs. So here goes:

Sign	Glyph	Manner
Aries	♈	Brave, courageous, impatient
Taurus	♉	Peaceful, stable, stubborn
Gemini	♊	Curious, young at heart, unreliable
Cancer	♋	Sensitive, emotional, moody
Leo	♌	Proud, creative, egotistical
Virgo	♍	Gentle, orderly, critical
Libra	♎	Charming, harmonious, false
Scorpio	♏	Intense, passionate, manipulative
Sagittarius	♐	Expansive, optimistic, grandiose
Capricorn	♑	Wise, conservative, fearful
Aquarius	♒	Innovative, original, extreme
Pisces	♓	Compassionate, intuitive, escapist

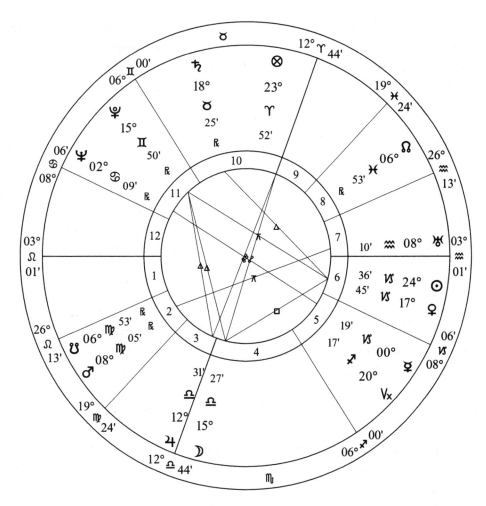

Joan of Arc
January 15, 1412 / 5:00 p.m. LMT / Domremy la Pucelle, France
Koch houses
Chart data from Kepler Version 7.0 Database, which states birth chart in hand, Stein-
brecher (www.astrosoftware.com).

In this book, I'll be referring to Joan of Arc's chart to help you identify certain points and concepts along the way. Don't think you need to be sainted in order to have a special soul purpose in your life. Remember that Joan of Arc was a simple peasant girl who made a big impact on the course of the Catholic Church. Her chart is on page 5.

Joan of Arc's planets are in the following signs:
Sun in Capricorn
Moon in Libra
Mercury in Capricorn
Venus in Capricorn
Mars in Virgo
Jupiter in Libra
Saturn in Taurus
Uranus in Aquarius
Neptune in Cancer
Pluto in Gemini

Everyone is born with the same toolkit of planets. Everyone's got a mental tool (Mercury), an emotional tool (the Moon), and so on. But the potential mix of planets in different signs is enough to make any statistics professor smile. So you can have two siblings born while the Sun was illuminating Cancer in different years, and they can be as different as night and day. Why? Maybe one has the Moon in lusty Leo, and the other has the Moon in secretive Scorpio. There's a mountain of information contained in your unique blend of planets in signs, but things get really interesting when we actually consult the map of the heavens for the precise moment of your birth, resulting in what is known as your birth chart. You can use the CD-ROM included with this book to run your chart.

Houses

When you look at your birth chart, the first thing you'll notice is that those glyphs are all over the place. Yep, get used to it. Fortunately, most charts come with a built-in legend that lays out the glyphs in plain English. The best way to understand what you're looking at is to imagine that your birth took place smack dab in the middle of the circle. If someone had taken a snapshot of the heavens at the moment of your birth, this is what it would look like astronomically.

So, if you're in the middle of the chart, then the top half of the chart corresponds to your view of the heavens, from eastern horizon to western horizon, at your birth. Chances are there are some planets positioned in the top half of your chart. Those particular planets were visible, either with the naked eye or with a telescope, at the time you were born.

The bottom half of the chart is the part of the sky that was not visible from your birth place. Just because you couldn't see those planets at the time of your birth doesn't mean that we don't count them in. In fact, because they are buried deep in the bottom of the chart, they tend to play their parts in an intensely personal way.

You've probably noticed that the circle is divided into twelve parts. These are traditionally called houses, which is not a very user-friendly term. These divisions of the chart represent different parts of your life, such as health or finances. Houses add a new dimension of information to your astrological profile because they are influenced by both the signs and the planets.

This may come as a surprise, but even if you were born while the Sun was in Cancer, you still have a bit of each sign in your makeup. The zodiac encircles your chart, just as it encircles the Earth. The exact time of your birth determines the sign that influences the starting point in your chart, otherwise known as your first house. In most cases, the next sign of the zodiac shows up on the doorway to the second house, and so on. You can identify the sign on any house by the glyph that falls on the line that separates each house from the previous house.

If a planet is positioned in a particular house, it adds its own special kind of energy to the goings-on of that part of your life. Let's say that upbeat Jupiter is placed in your relationship house (the seventh house). Jupiter's naturally optimistic, outgoing brand of energy will affect every one of your relationships, the good and the not so good.

Unlike signs and planets, there are no glyphs for the houses. They are simply numbered, one through twelve, in a counterclockwise direction. In contrast to the evenly divided 30° signs of the zodiac, a house can span significantly more or fewer than thirty degrees. In addition, there are all sorts of "house systems" that have been developed over the last several centuries. At this point in your studies, it's enough to know that there are different ways of slicing the astrological pie. The charts calculated in this book use the Koch house system, a relatively modern and increasingly popular system.

House	Part of Your Life
1	Physical body, persona
2	Money, earnings, values, self-worth
3	Education, neighborhood, siblings
4	Parents, family, home
5	Children
6	Work
7	Relationships
8	Life-changing experiences
9	Travel, religion
10	Career
11	Friends, future
12	Psychological strengths and weaknesses

Joan of Arc's planets are in the following houses:

Planet	House Placement
Sun in Capricorn	6
Moon in Libra	4
Mercury in Capricorn	5
Venus in Capricorn	6
Mars in Virgo	2
Jupiter in Libra	4
Saturn in Taurus	10
Uranus in Aquarius	7
Neptune in Cancer	11
Pluto in Gemini	11

By this point, you've probably figured out that a planet expresses its own special brand of energy in two different and distinct ways. The sign a planet falls in reflects how a planet expresses its nature. For example, Joan of Arc's Saturn is in Taurus. This suggests that she was determined to fulfill her karmic destiny come hell or, well, you get the picture.

The house placement identifies where she applied this consistently responsible part of her nature. In her case Saturn in Taurus falls in the tenth house, indicating that she would stubbornly hold to her values in the public arena in her life. In fact, she might even make a career of it, and her reputation would be based on her stalwart refusal to budge when it came to her beliefs.

Although the how and where of a planet's expression might seem pretty cut and dried, there are some similarities you should know about. Each of the twelve houses has a marked affinity for one of the zodiac signs. When a planet falls in a particular house, it takes on the look and feel of that house's favorite sign. Here's the cheat sheet for the house/sign exchange:

Planets in This House:	Will Act a Lot Like Planets in This Sign:
1	Aries
2	Taurus
3	Gemini
4	Cancer
5	Leo
6	Virgo
7	Libra
8	Scorpio
9	Sagittarius
10	Capricorn
11	Aquarius
12	Pisces

Each section of this book contains a separate paragraph for each sign/house combination. If you wanted to read more about Joan of Arc's Saturn in Taurus in the tenth house, you would look up two paragraphs. The first would be about Saturn in Taurus or the second house. Don't let the second-house part throw you—you'll understand in just a minute. Anyway, read the Saturn in Taurus paragraph, all the while remembering that the sign placement reflects how her Saturn does its job. Then turn to the paragraph about Saturn in the tenth house. The full title is actually "Saturn in Capricorn or the

Tenth House." This paragraph reveals where Joan's Saturn affects her life—in this case it affects her public life.

Yes, this does require some extra thought and analysis. In the long run, though, it provides much more information and awareness, whether you're working on your own chart or figuring out someone else's.

Aspects

Admittedly, this is where most folks' eyes cross. It's not your fault. We astrologers bandy about terms like "angular distance" and "orb" as if everyone should know exactly what we mean. Sure, there are plenty of technical terms to describe what an aspect is that will kick up any latent math anxiety, but you're not going to find that in this book. *Mapping Your Soul's Purpose* is about finding meaning in your life, not about taking another run at college calculus and logarithmic progressions.

Okay, now that that's out of the way, we can get down to business. "Aspects" is just a fancy word to describe cosmic connections and dialogue between two or more planets. Just as in life, some conversations are better than others. For instance, a loving exchange with your sweetie is a whole lot different than an ominous phone call from the IRS. Just keep that in mind, and you'll soon be a well-seasoned traveler on the aspect express.

In this book, we'll be using six different types of aspects to identify the cosmic commentary that is taking place deep down in your soul. Each aspect flavors the exchange between the two planets and enables you to integrate each planet into your life plan. Even so, some aspects have a bad reputation, and you'll do well to respect the positive potential as well as the destructive power inherent in any planetary conversation.

The first aspect is called a conjunction and occurs when two planets are right next to each other. Just like watercolors running together, conjunctions blend and blur the planets' energies together in your personality as well as your experience. Conjunctions naturally emphasize the sign and the house where they are located, and accentuate both the positive and negative attributes of the planets involved. In Joan of Arc's chart, the Libra Moon and Jupiter emphasize one another's nature. Jupiter's expansive qualities no doubt enhance her Moon's sensitivity and intuition. This takes place in the third house, the area of communication. Joan's message to the public was big, to say the least.

The next aspect is the opposition, and, just as it sounds, shows up when two planets fall on opposite sides of the chart. Unlike the emphasis of a conjunction, two planets opposing each other prompt you to integrate and include two very different parts of your nature and create a greater awareness. Oppositions force you to seek a healthy balance between the two opposed planets. There is a strong opposition between Joan of Arc's Mercury and Neptune, suggesting difficulty in expressing her spiritual beliefs or that her words might be misunderstood.

The aspect that cuts the circle into four quarters is called a square. Planets that square one another produce more than their fair share of friction in your life. But just like any good competition, squares bring out your best qualities if you're willing to face up to the challenge. The square between Joan's ambitious Venus in Capricorn and her peace-loving Libran Moon probably created plenty of internal conflict about whether she was doing the right thing. It also suggests a frustrated desire for tranquility pitched against an innate sense of duty and responsibility.

Trines create a stable triangle within the circle and promote a peaceful, easy feeling between the two connected planets. Most astrologers will tell you that trines are a beautiful thing, but they can also lead to complacency and laziness if you don't count your blessings and make the most of these gifts from the gods. Joan of Arc's sociable Moon and powerful Pluto are in a graceful connection that suggests an instinctive ease in dealing with those in elevated positions. Joan's relationship with King Charles VII of France, while unlikely given her own humble beginnings, changed the course of the Hundred Years War between France and England, not to mention the effect that she had on the Catholic religion.

Think of a sextile as half as good as a trine. With this aspect, you still have all the potential, but things don't flow quite as easily to you. You have to make a conscious decision to act on the opportunities presented by this pleasant planetary combination. Joan of Arc's chart does not contain any sextiles. It is quite common for a chart to lack one or more kinds of aspects. In Joan's case, the absence of sextiles does not indicate that her life lacked opportunity, for there are several avenues for certain conditions to show up in a chart.

A quincunx is just as hard to deal with as it is to say. In this enigmatic arrangement, two planets are bent on bringing their own agendas to the fore. Unfortunately, they lack any common characteristics and quite often end up in a tense standoff. There is a vague feeling that something is just not right. Interestingly, quincunxes introduce karmic themes and point to those parts of your nature that need to be adjusted and fine-tuned in this lifetime. Joan's chart shows an interesting quincunx between the cautious Venus in Capricorn and the curious Pluto in Gemini. Her conservative values may have seemed out of whack when compared with the powerful thoughts and ideas that emerged from her prayers, meditations, and spiritual guidance.

So, you might be asking yourself how often these conversations occur in a typical birth chart. The answer is lots. Each planet and house cusp is located at a specific address, or degree, in the zodiac, but aspects don't have to be right on the money. There's a certain amount of variance, called an orb, which makes it so that "almost" is just as good as "exact." In other words, if the planets are in the same neighborhood, they're close enough to be considered "in aspect." For example, if you are an adult, think back to when you were a teenager—you didn't have to be in the same room to get the message when your father was yelling at you to take out the trash. In Joan of Arc's chart, you'll notice that Venus is located at 17°46' Capricorn. While no other planets are at the exact same degree, Venus is still chatting it up with the Moon, Saturn, and Pluto.

One of the truly beautiful things about the information age is that computers do all of the math for you, and most computer charts provide a grid that illustrates each planet's relationship to the other planets in the chart. Orbs are another one of those contentious issues in astrology, and there are plenty of theories as to which set of orbs is the most accurate. Because this book has a specific focus, we'll be using smaller orbs than you might have seen in other books or programs. That's so you can concentrate on the most powerful karmic and spiritual factors in your own chart. Of course, as you continue your astrological studies, you'll want to experiment and explore other aspects and orbs. In the meantime, here are the aspects and orbs we'll be using in this book. Like planets and signs, aspects are represented by glyphs:

Aspect	Glyph	Meaning	Number of Degrees Apart	Orb
Conjunction	☌	Emphasis, combination	0°	4°
Opposition	☍	Awareness	180°	4°
Trine	△	Ease, harmony	120°	4°
Sextile	✶	Opportunity	60°	2°
Square	◻	Conflict, challenge	90°	4°
Quincunx	⚻	Adjustment	150°	2°

Now that we've covered the basics—planets, signs, houses, and aspects—you're ready to move on. If you haven't already done so, make sure to use the CD-ROM included with this book to create your own chart. It's your passport to explore your own soul's purpose. As you read each section, you'll notice that each topic contains a summary statement. These snapshot comments are cosmic clues that you can use to personalize each leg of your journey.

Just one final word: this book is best read start to finish. Sure, you'll still benefit if you give in to your inner Gemini and flit through the chapters in a haphazard way. If you resist that temptation and take the time to work through the information as it's laid out, you'll be amazed at the wonderful insights and understanding that will reward you for searching out your heart's desire and soul's intentions.

Part One
Rules for the Road

Where are you headed? How will you get there? What on earth did you have in mind for this lifetime? If you feel like you've been wandering in the desert, take heart. Your life is not just some random act of unassociated experiences and circumstances. Your chart reflects the perfect pattern that you set up long before you were born. In fact, you and your guides sat down and had some serious planning sessions about what great things you wanted to accomplish, as well as the challenges and obstacles you wanted to address in this life.

The first item on the agenda was to define your message and what you agreed to share with others and teach through your actions. The second item was to identify the primary lesson you need to learn and master in this life.

Astrologically and astronomically, these spiritually potent insights are reflected in the eclipses that occurred prior to your birth, called prenatal eclipses. Don't get hung up on this phrase. It's really just a fancy way to refer to a New Moon or Full Moon, which occur when the Sun, Moon, and Earth all line up in a row.

What this means to you is that in anticipation of your birth, the Sun and Moon also had a couple of important meetings. In one, they were in absolute agreement and shared the same opinion about your purpose and message. In the other, the Sun and the Moon opposed one another and had different but equally valid ideas about the lessons and challenges you must meet and overcome.

Before you read any further, take a moment to identify these important points in your chart:

- *Prenatal Solar Eclipse:* what you are here to teach others.
- *Prenatal Lunar Eclipse:* what you are here to learn from others.

While you're there, take note of the following points as well. We'll be covering them shortly.

- *The four directions, or angles, in your chart:*
    East—the Ascendant, or rising sign: your starting point.
    West—the Descendant, or setting sign: whom you want to partner up with.
    North—the IC, or nadir: who you are deep down in your soul.
    South—the Midheaven (MC), or zenith: what you want to accomplish.

To find out the signs that the two eclipses fell in before your birth, check out appendix 1 in the back of this book. Don't stop there. You can look up anyone's birthday to get a quick idea of what that person has to share and what challenges he or she faces. It may give you some nifty new insights into your partner, your boss, your kids, or even your in-laws. Just remember that this is pretty potent information, which can easily touch a raw nerve or two. So unless someone walks up to you and asks you to tell him what his lessons are, it's best to keep it under wraps.

The next thing that you mapped out prior to your birth was your personalized compass, so you can always figure out whether you are coming or going. Your chart is determined by the exact moment of your birth, so chances are, you gave some careful consideration to the layout of this lifetime. Just like a compass, you can use this helpful tool to figure out which direction to take in life, whether you're trying to find yourself, your soul mate, your history, or your destiny. Ultimately, your chart can guide you on a round-trip tour of your world and your potential, designed by and for you.

1
Prenatal Solar Eclipses
What You Are Here to Teach

The prenatal Solar Eclipse is just the ticket to understanding your strengths, your talents, and, more importantly, the ideas and ideals that you agreed to teach others through your actions. The nifty thing about this arrangement is that you really don't have to do a thing for others to learn from you. Just by being you, you can be assured that others are catching a clue.

As with all things astrological, you can do this in a positive way or a not-so-positive way. You can express the good or the bad, and folks will still come to the same conclusion. For example, let's say that your prenatal Solar Eclipse is in Aries, which means you are here to teach about taking action in your own self-interest. Now, your soul has a choice. You can play out the positive and set the standard in terms of asserting yourself in an appropriate way. Others look at you and say, "Gosh, I'm impressed. I want to act just like her!" Or, you can be a rageaholic, getting in everyone's face to the point that they stand up for themselves and tell you to take a hike. Either way, your mission is accomplished. However, you can bet the heavens would prefer that you take the high road, for the benefit and blessing of all concerned.

One more thing: You'll notice in this chapter that the headings for each Solar Eclipse reference a sign and a house. The sign of your prenatal Solar Eclipse tells you how to go about fulfilling your job in life, and the house points out in which part of your life all this karmic wheeling and dealing will take place. If you have your prenatal Solar Eclipse in Aries, first find the house where Aries shows up in your chart, and read the entry for that house. Let's say that Aries eclipse shows up in the second house, which is a money house. This means that you apply the Aries Solar Eclipse energy (teaching how to take appropriate action) to the second-house, or financial, part of your life. By referring to both factors, you get lots more information to work with. Use the eclipse tables in appendix 1 to find your own prenatal Solar Eclipse.

Prenatal Solar Eclipse in Aries or in the First House

I teach action.

You have made a pact with the heavens to share your innate bravado with those around you. Your ability to stand up and fight for what is right towers head and shoulders above the rest. Deep down, you are driven to conquer new territory, be assertive, and have the courage to follow your convictions.

First and foremost, though, you are driven to be first in everything, to take the first step, to be the head of the class, to shine brightly in the hearts and minds of those who love you. However, those you draw to you waver and waffle to the point that you can become uncertain of your direction. Even so, it's up to you to move into motion the moment you hear of the potential for new adventure.

Of course, you can play it safe and never make a move to leave your humble beginnings or venture into the big, wide world, but where's the fun in that? Hanging back out of harm's way still gets the message across to those around you: as you eek out an existence of quiet desperation, the folks watching you will eventually get the message that security isn't all it's cracked up to be.

Prenatal Solar Eclipse in Taurus or in the Second House

I teach perseverance.

When you signed on the bottom line, you agreed to teach the rest of us about the value of sticking with it, whatever it is. You're in it for the long haul, and you expect others to be also.

Your natural ability to dig in and bloom where you're planted is something that others marvel at, even obsess over. Partners can focus so much on capturing your sense of stability that they end up undermining your security. Ultimately, you must return to your solid sense of values in each of the three big parts of life: physical, emotional, and spiritual. The trick is to figure out what's worth sticking with and what needs to be released in order to move forward.

Of course, you can shirk the apparent boredom that comes from always being prepared and live life as though you don't have a care or obligation in the world, even after your mother loaned you the last of her retirement account. Just realize that when you create financial chaos in the lives of those around you, the message rings out loud and clear: get your money and your actions in sync, or you'll end up bankrupt, financially and spiritually.

Prenatal Solar Eclipse in Gemini or in the Third House

I teach curiosity.

What if you really could have your cake and eat it too? That and a hundred other questions stream through your consciousness and shape your everyday actions as you pursue the answers to the riddles in your head.

Your constant questing and questioning awaken others to the value of mental musing. You teach others to stop and smell the roses, chase the butterflies, and watch the sun set along the way. You take delight in the whimsical, and open your mind to the quirky and unusual experiences and instances that cross your path.

The minute you stop inquiring and investigating, you might as well pack your mind away in mothballs, for all the good it does you, or anyone else for that matter. Those folks who are waiting to learn about the importance of information will be sorely disappointed by your boring diatribes and dribble that all add up to "been there, done that." At any rate, the individuals who signed up for your Humanity 101 class will still get the message loud and clear: make a choice to learn and laugh along the way, and life will be that much sweeter.

Prenatal Solar Eclipse in Cancer or in the Fourth House

I teach emotional sensitivity.

This lifetime is all about the power of heartfelt love. You are on a first-name basis with all of the major emotions: love, fear, joy, and sorrow. What sets you apart from the rest of humankind is that you comprehend that emotions are processes rather than death sentences. So, instead of hesitancy and trepidation, you embrace the full spectrum of feelings with emotional security and maturity.

Being able to ride the tide of ever changing sentiments is not exactly child's play. And yet, you attract some of the most selfish, childish, insensitive brutes on the block. You chose to teach the benefits of emotional wisdom, and many of your relationships turn into classrooms in which you instruct your partner on how to identify, acknowledge, and act on his or her own emotional cues and clues.

There's always plan B, in which you turn a cold shoulder toward even your closest confidants. Once you've established yourself as the Wicked Witch of the West, the souls around you will still have learned that there's no place like home and that heart and soul are inextricably linked.

Prenatal Solar Eclipse in Leo or in the Fifth House

I teach creativity.

In the midst of all this serious spiritual stuff, it may sound kind of silly, but you are here to teach others how to have fun and how to stay enchanted with the world. While that particular karmic responsibility may earn a scoff or two from your business-minded Capricorn pals, the truth is that the heart of all creative endeavors is joy. In other words, if whatever you're doing doesn't make your light shine, then maybe it isn't worth doing.

Your relationships are littered with those who are forever frozen in the paralysis of analysis. Others are attracted to your excitement and passion. Even so, they stubbornly stick to the idea that they can never join in the dance of life. At this point it becomes next to impossible for them to shatter the pattern of detachment and indifference that stalls their own soul's progress.

Of course, you can be won over by the logic that life is not to be filled with one passionate dance after another. Eventually, your own spinning top will come to a dull and complete stop. Then, others in your life will mutter and murmur as to why, exactly, you didn't follow your heart's desire, while uttering a silent prayer that they, themselves, will ultimately create a life to be proud of.

Prenatal Solar Eclipse in Virgo or in the Sixth House

I teach order.

Your particular mission in this lifetime is to teach others to get their act together. You have a knack for order and organization, and are able to assess and analyze the most perplexing of problems. Your antennae are always up and scanning the airwaves for errors and inaccuracies, and you make no bones about the fact that proper sequence and succession are as much a part of the soul's code as prayer and devotion.

You've dedicated this lifetime to teaching others how to master the finer points of method and means. Those you draw into your experience, however, quite often lack even the most rudimentary understanding of the real world, and the rules and regulations that go with it. You quite often find yourself hooked up with some mighty messy and malevolent characters.

While it may be tempting to throw caution and care to the wind in favor of all-out foolishness, you couldn't pull it off very well. After all, can you really picture yourself looking at life through rose-colored glasses as your credit score plummets and your cholesterol goes sky high? Let's say you did—as you scattered your life force to the four winds, the spectators in your life would still get the message: a life lived without conscious commitment and dedication goes nowhere.

Prenatal Solar Eclipse in Libra or in the Seventh House

I teach awareness of others.

Moving into this lifetime, you brought with you a clear understanding of pairing and partnering. Your natural charm and grace open the door to many relationships, and others are fascinated by your apparent ease in interacting in any number of interesting situations. Your innate awareness of the give and take of partnerships is a great gift, and you find yourself instructing others on the real meaning of having and holding. Throughout your lifetime, your capacity to hook up and hold on shows others that the key to moving forward spiritually is to make peace, not war.

That's not to say that you can't raise a hand or raise your voice when you need to. While you have a crystal-clear vision of the perfect partner, chances are your sweetie has more than a few rough edges. In fact, it is in your own partnerships that your capacity to assert your desires is most called upon, and yet, even then, others will view your actions as elegant and poised.

Of course, you can occasionally go over to the dark side of anger and antagonism and create such an intense aura of confrontation around your life that others will beg to be set free. While that may not be the most enlightened way to teach peace, others in your life will still learn the lesson that love and peace, beauty and bliss, are high but attainable ideals.

Prenatal Solar Eclipse in Scorpio or in the Eighth House

I teach intensity.

As you prepared for this lifetime, you imagined yourself crafting a meaningful existence while teaching others how to wield their own strength and spiritual power. In reality, that is exactly what you are doing, but it may not be in the straightforward way that your soul had hoped for. In fact, experience has probably taught you that surrendering to others' agendas and expectations is a mucky, murky swamp that can dilute the most potent of desires. And so, again and again, you return to the most elementary of Scorpion creeds: get to the point.

Rather than honoring their own strength and embracing their power to transform their lives into something truly divine, your partners project onto you their own angst over the inevitability of change. They whine, moan, and shake their fists at the heavens in a melodramatic plea for life to stay the same, all the while implying that you and your piercing insights are what started the whole problem. But change they must, and the only thing that will jinx it is if you step in and try to assume the alterations for them.

At times, you long for peace and are tempted to try for a kinder, gentler existence. Just be warned that one peaceful, placid day looks pretty much like all the others, and the boredom will kill you. As you are being laid to rest, you and everyone around you will whisper and wonder about whatever happened to your razor-sharp intensity.

Prenatal Solar Eclipse in Sagittarius or in the Ninth House

I teach exploration.

After lifetimes of being on the road, wandering around the big, wide, wonderful world, you have a traveler's savvy that you're more than willing to share with friend and stranger alike. The fact is you can make yourself at home anywhere, so there's no real fear in crossing the road or crossing the border as long as you've packed your bags with your insatiable curiosity and your desire to acquire new experiences and understanding.

As far as relationships go, your bags are packed but you just might miss the boat, because your beloved would much rather take a quick spin around the neighborhood as opposed to circumnavigating the globe. Even then, your partner isn't necessarily open to your broad-minded views and fascination with all things foreign.

Interestingly, you can get distracted and lose your ability to find true north. Worse yet, you can end up drudging through daily tasks and droning on about doctrine and dogma with an absolute absence of open-mindedness or ongoing quest for truth. Even then, your actions and attitudes inspire those around you to set off for parts and philosophies unknown, if for no other reason than to escape your pompous ponderings.

Prenatal Solar Eclipse in Capricorn or in the Tenth House

I teach responsibility.

Your contract with the heavens is to take yourself and your obligations seriously and to apply your own brand of savvy to any situation. You have an innate understanding of the spiritual bottom line. You are well aware that unless you fulfill your responsibilities and live up to your word, your life won't add up to much at all. Sure, that sounds cold and harsh, but this stark contrast compels others to break out of their own mediocre existence and reach for a life worth living.

A partner who understands your commitment to manifesting a better life would be an incredible asset. Thank your lucky stars when that does happen, because your encounters with such people will be few and far between. Instead, you find that your own level of success attracts those who are burdened by immense emotional baggage and who need you to create a safe haven in which their own drama of tears and fears can take center stage. Fortunately, your common sense can help you avoid taking responsibility for other people's emotional lessons.

At times, you can become so weary that shirking your responsibilities and abandoning your achievements seems like the only way out. As others view the fallout of that conduct, they will turn away with a greater sense of resolve to own up to their own duties. These actions will still teach others the significance of responsibility, but your spirit will lose the sense of satisfaction that comes from a life well lived.

Prenatal Solar Eclipse in Aquarius or in the Eleventh House

I teach independence.

Your commitment to the cosmos is to arouse and inspire the sleeping dragon of independence and individuality in others. You definitely march to the beat of a different, distant drummer, and your eyes are always looking toward the horizon to identify what's next and what's new in your life. While some would call you a rogue or a rebel, you understand and adhere to some of the fundamental laws of life, including the necessity for long-range planning.

You would like nothing better than a friend or close companion to accompany you on your journey, but instead your partners are quite often opposed to your path as well as your newfangled ideas. Their fixed ideas and gigantic egos create huge obstacles, but only if you lose perspective of what is important to you.

At times, you can sink into crazy passions and seek to dictate the thoughts and actions of those around you. Of course, this will only lead to their rebellion when they demand the right to think for themselves and create their own future. While this will still satisfy your obligation to the heavens, your soul will truly mourn the loss of understanding and objectivity.

Prenatal Solar Eclipse in Pisces or in the Twelfth House

I teach compassion.

In this lifetime, your sacred covenant is to inspire others to have undying faith and devotion to the belief that our collective thoughts, beliefs, and philosophies define and describe our relationships with each other and with the divine. Your great ability to be both artistic and intuitive is to be shared with anyone and everyone as you move through your life and times. However, your greatest asset, the ability to comprehend the depths and darkness of the human soul and still extend compassion, is the crucial cornerstone of your contribution.

You long for unconditional love, for love that looks beyond the physical and searches for the metaphysical within the bonds of partnership. Unfortunately, those you draw to you are often critical, judgmental, and fixed upon the imperfect form and structure of life rather than the perfection of spirit. It is within this stressful environment that you are forced to see and seek your own truth.

At times, you can lose your way and find yourself perfecting the prickly and persnickety side of your nature. Before you know it, you're fussing and fretting over being loved in the perfect way while your friends and lovers implore you to be kinder, gentler, and more forgiving. While that may enable you to consider your contract completed, it will do little to soothe your gentle soul as it returns to the search for heaven on earth.

2
Prenatal Lunar Eclipses
What You Are Here to Learn

As you read through the information for your prenatal Lunar Eclipse, you'll notice a couple of things. One is that it sounds a lot more challenging than the prenatal Solar Eclipse. It is. The other is that if you've been paying attention to the patterns in your life, it sounds all too familiar.

The good news is that the sign of your prenatal Lunar Eclipse tells you all about the building blocks that comprise your life lessons. It also informs you about the quality and nature of teachers that cross your path. These can be nice or not so nice. For example, let's say that your prenatal Lunar Eclipse is in Libra, which means you are here to learn about forming real relationships. Of course, you will encounter those who easily overpower you as you try to acquiesce and play fair. That's just no fun, so eventually you will walk away, shaking your fist at the heavens and saying never again. Occasionally, you will run across someone who honors and respects you. Either scenario will teach you about what you do and don't want in the world of relationships. Even better, the more you work on the lessons of your prenatal Lunar Eclipse, the fewer dirty rotten scoundrels will cross your path.

You'll notice in this chapter that the headings for each prenatal Lunar Eclipse reference a sign and a house. The sign of your Lunar Eclipse tells you how you go about learning your lessons, and the house tells you in which part of your life this takes place. So, if your prenatal Lunar Eclipse is in Libra, first find the house where Libra shows up in your chart, and read the entry for that house. Let's say that Libra eclipse shows up in your second house, which is a money house. This means that you apply that Libra Lunar Eclipse energy (learning how to form appropriate relationships) to the financial part of your life. So, by referring to both factors, you get lots of insight and guidance. Use the eclipse tables in appendix 1 to find your own prenatal Lunar Eclipse.

Prenatal Lunar Eclipse in Aries or in the First House

I learn about myself.

Aries energy is all about defining who you are, both to yourself and to others through your actions. Chances are that you have spent lifetimes fussing and fretting over your significant others to the point that their personalities eclipsed your own. As you entered this life, you decided that you need to learn a whole lot more about what lights your fire. You want to use some of that inner bravado to fight for your own rights, for a change.

It would certainly be helpful if the gods and cosmos put you in a situation in which everyone around you honored your true-blue nature and prompted you to do what is best for yourself. However, these brothers in arms are few and far between. Instead, you find that you are often surrounded by dependent folks who readily rely upon you for direction and the basic necessities of life. Eventually, you must honor your anger and impatience to break free, as this is the only way to reach the core of courage to be yourself.

To win the Aries battle, you must be willing to look out for number one, because if you wait around for others to take care of you, you will quickly find yourself on the losing side of the war. Instead, you must combine intention with action and forge ahead in nearly every area of your life.

Make sure to pay special attention to the connections between Mars and the other players in your chart. Easy connections make it more comfortable to integrate this lesson, whereas the tough connections are bound to create obstacles and challenges along your spiritual path.

Prenatal Lunar Eclipse in Taurus or in the Second House

I learn about values.

In Utopia, everyone's necessities would be miraculously provided, and want and need would all but be abolished. Yes, that would be nice, but that kind of magical day-dreaming does not pay the electric bill. In this lifetime, you decided to sign up for Money 101 to learn the ins and outs of finances, setting priorities, determining your value system, and defining your own self-worth.

Over and over again, you will be faced with the difficult lesson of earning and learning the value of a dollar and determining your own self-worth as well. This does not automatically mean that you will live a life of poverty. In fact, you may be quite comfortable, to the point that you are not sure where you begin and where your job title or portfolio ends. That's what the Taurus lesson is all about—taking the time to weigh and measure your own worth against all of the things that can and will possess you.

To truly benefit from the Taurus lesson, you must acknowledge and honor the physical facts of your existence. You must count your blessings, as well as the money in your bank account. Most importantly, you need to revel in the sheer luxury of the senses and take time to smell the roses along life's path.

Make sure to pay special attention to the connections between Venus and the other players in your chart. Easy connections make it more comfortable to integrate the lessons of Taurus, whereas the tough connections are bound to create obstacles and challenges along your spiritual path.

Prenatal Lunar Eclipse in Gemini or in the Third House

I learn about options.

Gemini's role in the scheme of things is to offer up a plethora of options and opportunities as well as the ability to have your cake and eat it too. After lifetimes filled to the brim with the same old thing, day in and day out, your soul opted to take a holiday and open up to the ever changing kaleidoscope of ideas and experiences that dot the Gemini landscape.

Unfortunately, most folks around you simply don't understand your driving desire to take pleasure in the various delights that the garden of life has to offer. Instead, your traveling companions endeavor to strip your wings, enforce some kind of curfew, and pray to heaven that you'll settle down and get a job. Of course, you can go along with them and find yourself beating your wings against the glass ceiling of a conventional life. Or—and here's where the challenge of Gemini's choices really begins to hit home—you can honor your inner wanderer and embrace the value of experience as much, if not more, than accomplishment.

The lesson contained in Gemini is to set your mind free from conventional thinking and leave no stone unturned, no matter how politically incorrect your innocent ponderings may seem. You are here to relearn a childlike delight that you lost lifetimes ago. So go ahead and question yourself, your world, and everything in it. It is in that search for answers and understanding that your mind will expand and your soul will smile at the wonder of it all.

Make sure to pay special attention to the connections between Mercury and the other players in your chart. Easy connections make it more comfortable to integrate the lessons of Gemini, whereas the tough connections are bound to create obstacles and challenges along your spiritual path.

Prenatal Lunar Eclipse in Cancer or in the Fourth House

I learn sensitivity.

Cancer is all about the world of emotions, feelings, tenderness, and nurturing. As you were setting up your objectives in this lifetime, these were high on your list. You decided, based on your experiences in past lives, that you needed to learn about the finer points of sensitivity. You must accept and acknowledge your own needs and emotions and also create supportive relationships in your life.

A Cancer Lunar Eclipse suggests that while you are learning the delicate balance between cynicism, sensitivity, and sacrifice, you might attract other souls who will gently mentor you in this unfamiliar classroom. However, this cosmic factor frequently delivers needy, whiny, childish folks who challenge your resolve to be sensitive. In fact, these hangers-on that suck you dry are actually the heavens' way of backing you into a corner and forcing you to figure out what you need and how to get it. The good news is that the more you honor your own needs, as well as the needs of others, the more you will attract the souls into your life who will do the same for you.

In order to honor your Cancer Lunar Eclipse, you must learn to nourish yourself and your soul. That doesn't mean cramming a fast-food burger down in two minutes between taking your spouse's suits to the cleaners and meeting with your son's preschool teacher. Instead, you must actively and honestly acknowledge that you need things too.

Make sure to pay special attention to the connections between the Moon and the other players in your chart. Easy connections make it more comfortable to integrate the lessons of Cancer, whereas the tough connections are bound to create obstacles and challenges along your spiritual path.

Prenatal Lunar Eclipse in Leo or in the Fifth House

I learn about creative passion.

Leo reflects your soul's innate capacity to create for passion's sake. Leo is at the very heart of any creative endeavor and warms you to the core of your being. At least, that's the plan. But learning to let go and have fun is not as easy as it sounds, especially since you've spent lifetimes so focused on the future that you zoned out of the here and now. However, you've set things up differently in this lifetime, and every circumstance and relationship will lead you to recognize one simple truth: that you must actively and purposely choose a passionate life, or it will simply pass you by.

The unconventional nature of your pals and partners certainly stimulates your mind and offers up plenty of unusual ways to pass the time. However, you need to be careful of becoming so involved in their cases and causes that you end up empty-handed, lacking the heart and spirit to create a life to be proud of.

To embrace the Leo lesson, you must make time for fun and games. Explore your creative nature, and open up to the ideas and inspiration that stream steadily through the cosmos and into your consciousness. Learn to honor your own creations, whatever they are, and discover that an occasional indulgence warms your heart and soul.

Make sure to pay special attention to the connections between the Sun and the other players in your chart. Easy connections make it more comfortable to integrate the lessons of Leo, whereas the tough connections are bound to create obstacles and challenges along your spiritual path.

Prenatal Lunar Eclipse in Virgo or in the Sixth House

I learn about honoring my physical world.

In ancient times, Virgo was associated with the harvest, and as a result, has a strong association with the practical necessities of life. After lifetimes in which you were submerged in a sea of spirituality and surrendered your sense of self, your soul probably thought that it was well past time to come back down to earth.

The gift of Virgo is the ability to discern, to separate the wheat from the chaff. This turns out to be a real blessing, considering the state of your relationships. Because of your incredible capacity to forgive and forget, folks treat you in the most abominable fashion. Sure, you can sacrifice yourself in a mythical quest to save their souls, or you can recognize that their actions are unacceptable and that you must draw a line in the sand to preserve your sanity, not to mention your bank account and well-being.

To utilize the Virgo lesson, you must respect the realities of your existence. Stop wandering in and out of jobs and praying for manna from heaven to sustain you. Instead, just like the Virgo of old, you have to make hay while the sun shines, put away for a rainy day, and eat your vegetables.

Make sure to pay special attention to the connections between Mercury and the other players in your chart. Easy connections make it more comfortable to integrate the lessons of Virgo, whereas the tough connections are bound to create obstacles and challenges along your spiritual path.

Prenatal Lunar Eclipse in Libra or in the Seventh House

I learn about partnership.

Libra is all about the perplexing world of partners and partnerships. Ultimately, Libra is a journey, forcing you to peer into the looking glass of interaction and compare and contrast your own nature with that of your potential partner.

The blessing of Libra is the ability to be objective and to create win-win solutions. Your past lives were filled with courage and conquests, and you no doubt strode into this lifetime confident that you could quickly and easily command the world of relationships as well. However, your partnerships have not exactly been harmonious and blissful. Instead, you seem to draw those who raise your hackles, and before you know it, your hand is on your sword and you are ready to send them packing.

As you learn to incorporate Libra's longing for peace and tranquility into your life, you must first find peace within yourself. Create a life of balance and harmony. Learn to assert yourself without being aggressive. Take time to relax and enjoy the finer things of life, without the trauma and drama of constant conflict.

Make sure to pay special attention to the connections between Venus and the other players in your chart. Lots of easy connections make it more comfortable to integrate the lessons of Libra, whereas the tough connections are bound to create obstacles and delays along your spiritual path.

Prenatal Lunar Eclipse in Scorpio or in the Eighth House

I learn about intensity.

In Scorpio's deep, dark tangle of edgy intensity, it's easy to get caught up in the quest for control. That's a perfectly normal instinct, but Scorpio forces you to evolve and reminds you of your deep desire to thrive instead of just survive.

Survival is what your past lives were all about. Most likely, you focused on controlling risk and growth to the point that life became one predictable episode after another. Oh sure, you were safe and sound, but just because you were living didn't mean that your soul was alive with pleasure.

The good news is that Scorpio awakens your spirit with a craving for love and lust and all that other good stuff thrown in. You may wonder if there is a method to the madness, as you are frequently plunged into the deep end of the ocean without a life jacket. It is in the stark intensity when your life or marriage or portfolio or career hangs in the balance that you realize your own strength.

Most likely, your friends and lovers won't see it that way. Chances are you'll attract the type who wants nothing more than a little cottage with a white picket fence and who will whine and moan every step of the way as you search for deep, meaningful experiences.

Make sure to pay special attention to the connections between Pluto and the other players in your chart. Lots of easy connections make it more comfortable to integrate the lessons of Scorpio, whereas the tough connections are bound to create obstacles and delays along your spiritual path.

Prenatal Lunar Eclipse in Sagittarius or in the Ninth House

I learn about freedom.

Sagittarius reminds you that if life is not a daring adventure, it's nothing at all. For any adventure to begin or continue, freedom of both thought and action must be part of the game plan. Without either or both, you simply talk big and go nowhere. On the other hand, when both are in place, there is simply no chasm too wide or mountain too high for you to reach the highest heights of human consciousness.

Sounds impressive, doesn't it? Almost too impressive. Well, Sagittarius originated the concept of "bigger, better, faster, stronger," and takes great pride in its bragging rights for over-the-top, larger-than-life experiences. That's just what your soul ached for as it shopped around for learning experiences in this lifetime. You yearned to learn to explore your world and expand your philosophy of love, life, and everything else, for that matter.

No doubt, this free-spiritedness sprang from the frustration of one too many lifetimes living and dying in the same house and never venturing more than ten miles from home. Sure, you got to know your neighbors and your neighborhood like the back of your hand. You all knew each others' tired tales long before you set one foot into the grave, all the while craving adventure and passion.

Fortunately, Sagittarius is just the ticket to get out of Dodge. The lesson lies in the fact that Sagittarius tempts and taunts you well out of your comfort zone and way, way out on a limb. It is in this focused moment, when you realize you can't go home again, that your soul is freed to experience life as one exciting adventure after another.

Make sure to pay special attention to the connections between Jupiter and the other players in your chart. Lots of easy connections make it more comfortable to integrate the lessons of Sagittarius, whereas the tough connections are bound to create obstacles and delays along your spiritual path.

Prenatal Lunar Eclipse in Capricorn or in the Tenth House

I learn about accomplishment.

Capricorn's reputation is built on a rock-solid foundation of care and caution, conscientiousness and concern. Not exactly light and fluffy, but if you want to do great things, there is usually a great deal of work and sweat involved.

This is not to say that all of your lessons are serious and that your life experiences are bound to be tough and tedious. There is a lot of pleasure to be derived from a life well lived, from the simple sweetness of success, from the wealth of wisdom derived from knowing yourself and being true to your ambitions.

After lifetimes of navigating oceans of emotion, sacrificing your own sense of self, and nurturing countless others, your soul was ready for a chance to put all of those abilities to work in a more productive way. That's not to say that you've given up on being kind and gentle—not at all. But just like a displaced homemaker, you're ready to see how well you'll do in the "real world."

Your relationships with others force you to assess the consequences of any given course of action, and you have the unenviable task of pointing out the realities of the situation, despite your own feelings.

The good news is that buried deep in the bedrock of Capricorn is the secret to your success. As you settle in to learn the clear-cut rules of the road, Capricorn will reveal the tried and true path to achieve your highest ambitions on your own terms.

Make sure to pay special attention to the connections between Saturn and the other players in your chart. Lots of easy connections make it more comfortable to integrate the lessons of Capricorn, whereas the tough connections are bound to create obstacles and delays along your spiritual path.

Prenatal Lunar Eclipse in Aquarius or in the Eleventh House

I learn about individuality.

When folks talk about marching to the beat of a different drummer, have you ever considered just who was tinkering and toying with the rhythm of life? The essence of Aquarius is like a frustrated teenager rebelling against the sing-song reasoning of his or her parents and teachers. The inherent innovation of Aquarius is bound to ruffle a few conservative feathers as it unleashes radically new ideas and advocates the role of the individual in the network of society.

Heady stuff. Yes, you signed up for the advanced-thinking class in this lifetime, and your spirit is ready to take flight. All you have to do is open up to a new attitude that different is good and experimentation is the ultimate experience.

That's where your past and your partners can seriously complicate things. In past lives, you were focused on creating only what you could control and what ultimately increased your reputation. While you may have been successful, your megalomania may have made you just a little bit lonely. So now you're interested in pals and partners who will really shake things up and help you break these old patterns of the past. However, many of the people you draw to you are simply pulling your strings and pushing your buttons, watching you jerk from one response to another. Ultimately, you have to free yourself and learn to look at the big picture, whether it's concerning a partnership or a project.

Aquarius is like a fresh breeze ruffling your hair and cooling your brow on a scorching summer day. It reminds you to breathe deep, step back, and lighten up. As you're cooling off in the shade, chances are you'll link up with others who change and challenge your views until you truly can see yourself and the cosmos in one incredible panoramic perspective.

Make sure to pay special attention to the connections between Uranus and the other players in your chart. Lots of easy connections make it more comfortable to integrate the lessons of Aquarius, whereas the tough connections are bound to create obstacles and delays along your spiritual path.

Prenatal Lunar Eclipse in Pisces or in the Twelfth House

I learn about faith.

Just because Pisces is the last sign of the zodiac doesn't mean it's the end of the road, karmically speaking, anyway. Pisces is about having the faith to descend into the spooky depths of the subconscious and purifying your soul in the process. Pisces invites you into the realm of the mystical and magical and reminds you that the world of make-believe is just as viable as the cold, hard realities of the here and now.

On a soul level, you chose to learn to navigate by inner light and intuition. After trudging through lifetimes filled with duty and drudgery, you opted to escape into the gentle rhythm of a life unscripted. Nowhere in life does the need to heed your sixth sense show up more than in the quicksand of relationships. This placement draws in the liars and dirty rotten scoundrels who fake their way into the inner sanctum of your trust. The challenge is to learn when to believe what your senses are telling you and when you need to look past your own tendency to criticize and analyze the other person—a delicate balance indeed.

The true gift of Pisces is the capacity to see the good and god in everyone and everything. As you learn to show compassion, both to yourself and to others, the blessing of being able to forgive and forget will flow through your life and times with ease. Once you are able to see the perfection of life in progress, the romantic vision of Pisces can finally come out to play, painting your world with beauty and bliss, grace and light.

Make sure to pay special attention to the connections between Neptune and the other players in your chart. Lots of easy connections make it more comfortable to integrate the lessons of Pisces, whereas the tough connections are bound to create obstacles and delays along your spiritual path.

3
The Compass in Your Chart
Finding True North

Your chart is actually a map of the circumstances and situations in your life. Like any map, it contains important guideposts to help you reach your final destination. You've probably noticed by now that your chart is sliced up into twelve pieces. The different sections of your chart encompass all of life's experiences, from money to matrimony, kids to career. By the way, the astrologese term for these divisions of the chart is *houses*. These parts of your chart describe the situations and circumstances of your life. Houses are *where* the planets and signs converge in your chart. Despite their old-fashioned name, houses really do help you discover how you fit into the world around you.

The Ascendant/Descendant

There are four houses that pack a lot bigger punch than the rest of the houses. In fact, they are so powerful that they are referred to by special names rather than just their house numbers. The first two power houses that illuminate your path are the first and seventh houses. The special name for the cusp of the first house is the *Ascendant*.

Another name for it is the *rising sign*. Think of it as your starting point in this lifetime. It helps clarify your intentions at the beginning of your journey.

The seventh-house cusp is called the *Descendant*, or the *setting sign*. It's really the undiscovered country in your chart and feels a bit foreign, but secretly you're fascinated by it. This part of your chart lures and tempts you into the looking glass of relationships and forces you to become aware of the differences and, more importantly, the similarities between you and the other people in your life.

As you become more familiar with astrology, you'll come to appreciate its patterns and symmetry. For example, if you have an Aries Ascendant, you automatically have a Libra Descendant. Is that easy and convenient, or what?

Aries Ascendant/Libra Descendant

I project bravado, but I seek confirmation.

You seem to meet the world head-on, unfettered by doubts about the certainty of your success or the wisdom of your actions. You are ready to go at a moment's notice and dive into any activity or cause that lights your fire. You blaze ahead, leaving the cleanup and follow-through for others.

On a soul level, you decided that this lifetime was about fighting your own battles, rather than spilling your blood on behalf of others. Your karmic lessons lead you back to the crucial truth that you can't wrestle with anyone's dragons but your own.

On the other hand, you didn't really sign up for a life of solitude and quiet contemplation. Libra infuses you with the desire to share your life and times. However, you must learn to balance your longing for love and adoration with this lifetime's lesson to love and honor yourself as much as you love those who share your path.

Taurus Ascendant/Scorpio Descendant

I project stability, but I seek change.

As you consciously chose this incarnation, you decided to project the very essence of dependability and capability, caution and practicality. Slow and steady wins the race and you have every intention of not only winning the race but reaching the highest level of success as well.

On a soul level, you decided that this lifetime was about putting your capacity for consistency to good use and creating a rock-solid sense of self. Your karmic lessons lead you back to the fundamental truths that the only person you can really depend on is you and the best return on your investment is the time and energy invested in yourself.

Deep down, you crave a partner who will challenge your stubborn beliefs and dare you to dig yourself out of any well-worn ruts. However, you must balance your yearning for change with this lifetime's lesson to remain steadfast to your own values in the wake of the turmoil that others bring to your door.

Gemini Ascendant/Sagittarius Descendant

I project diversity, but I seek focus.

Clever and witty, you never fail to fascinate others as you flit and flutter effortlessly from one escapade to another. Your senses are constantly scanning your surroundings, and you are on a lifelong quest for a true meeting of the minds.

After lifetimes of being locked up in the castle keep, you decided you wanted to be a man (or woman) about town, with places to go and people to see. Your karmic lessons lead you back to the essential awareness that despite society's expectations, you are here to gather an abundance of experiences, as opposed to accomplishments.

Because you already look at life through stereoscopic lenses, relationships are complex because they add a third viewpoint to the mix. Partners help you focus and free you from scattering your energy in too many directions. Even so, you must learn to curb your secret appetite for single-mindedness, and honor that part of you that simply loves to listen and learn as you make your way down the road.

Cancer Ascendant/Capricorn Descendant

I project sensitivity, but I seek structure.

To say that you feel your way through life is a vast understatement. Tender and responsive, you easily move and maneuver through the emotional hills and valleys where others fear to tread.

After one too many lifetimes ending up as Old Mother Hubbard, your soul is on a mission to acknowledge and address your own needs, for a change. These are not easy tasks, considering you are constantly submerged in a supersensitive sea of others' needs and expectations. However, your karmic lessons consistently confirm that you really need to nurture your own personal agenda.

Is it any wonder that you are privately mesmerized by the cornerstone of Capricorn confidence and self-assurance? While living on solid ground may seem inviting, you will always be a child of the ocean of emotion. The great lesson here is to realize that the cool and calculated savvy of Capricorn is not a replacement for your sympathetic style, but rather a lovely accompaniment to your enchanting emotional outlook.

Leo Ascendant/Aquarius Descendant

I project passion, but I seek objectivity.

Loud and proud, no one can deny your presence as you enter the room to make a warm and lasting impression. You look at your life as a grand romantic epic, with you playing the conquering hero on a divine quest to create your own king- or queendom.

Spiritually, you decided that this lifetime was for passionately pursuing your heart's desire. Armed with a bounty of nobility, confidence, generosity, and a touch of drama, you're able to fake it till you make yourself into a genuine success story, worthy of accolades and adoration. If you fall prey to flattery, your karmic lesson kicks in and reminds you that you're not here to lay your own ideals aside for the good of humanity. Instead, you are here to inspire and arouse others as you follow your bliss.

On the other hand, a life of feverish creativity can burn out even the brightest star. Aquarius offers crystal-clear insight and logic, reason and rationale, and your partners provide a welcome respite from the overwhelming drives that demand your constant attention.

Virgo Ascendant/Pisces Descendant

I project practicality, but I seek solace.

Instead of meeting and greeting life head-on, you stand back and observe in an effort to map out the most efficient way to live your life and conquer your karma—a wholesome and holy intention.

After lifetimes of cleaning up others' messes, you decided this life was your chance to create order out of the chaos of your past lives. However, your plan can quickly go awry as you look around this perfectly imperfect world. This incarnation is for using your capacity to evaluate and assess, to judge what's right for you, instead of judging others.

The temptation to succumb to the still, deep waters of Pisces is always present as its mystical music soothes your inner critic. Go ahead and immerse yourself in the gentle ebb and flow, as Pisces blurs the boundaries and invites your inner skeptic to have faith. Pisces is a nice place to visit, but you wouldn't want to live there. However, you can take the beautiful dreams and visions with you as you move your body and soul through the mundane motions of life in progress.

Libra Ascendant/Aries Descendant

I project peace, but I desire excitement.

Your first response to the world was a question: How and where do I fit in? Ever since then, life has been one balancing act after another. Relationships are easy enough to come by, chiefly because you're more than willing to acquiesce in your search for approval and acknowledgment.

Relationships of every kind overshadowed your true nature in past incarnations, but you have decided to balance the scales and seek justice for yourself this time around. That's why every relationship reaches a critical crossroads where you must choose between codependence and independence.

You see yourself as the great peacemaker, and yet you are drawn to those most likely to create disruption and unrest. Aries here suggests that it's prime time for you to be your true self with your pals and partners. In fact, the gods and cosmos drive the point home that problems will continue to plague you until you confront them, as well as your own role in relationships, directly.

Scorpio Ascendant/Taurus Descendant

I project control, but I seek pleasure.

You rise up to meet the world with a watchful wariness unmatched by any other sign. Silent and still, you study and scrutinize those who cross your path and, more importantly, anyone who crosses you.

Deep down, on a soul level, you decided that this lifetime was about gaining control over yourself and your life force. You chose the most intense route available to define and refine your strength and skills. Karmically, though, you have to put all that impressive power to good use and transcend the chaotic circumstances that litter your life. Otherwise, you will find yourself on a treadmill of tiresome tedium, mastering one incline after another.

In the midst of all this upheaval, the rock-solid security of Taurus stands out like a beacon of hope. Even the quiet monotony is a balm to your spirit. However, Taurus teaches that you must not allow your constant craving for peace and predictability to obscure the authentic passions of your soul.

Sagittarius Ascendant/Gemini Descendant

I project know-how, but I seek information.

You greet the world straight as an arrow, with a bold sense of purpose and an un-abashed assurance that you will reach your target, no matter how far or difficult it is to achieve. You look at life as an adventure and emphatically believe that freedom of thought and action is a god-given right.

On a soul level, you decided that this lifetime was about expanding your conscious-ness and exploring your world. You challenge others with your flair for forward thinking and seeing well into the wild blue yonder. Over and over again, your karmic lessons em-phasize the fundamental truth that the journey is just as important as the destination.

On the other hand, this doesn't mean that you're always supposed to be getting out of Dodge. Adventures wait just around the corner, and Gemini is just the sign to lead you on a delightful journey through the neighborhood. Flitting to and fro can quickly sap your strength and distract you from the driving passions that stir within.

Capricorn Ascendant/Cancer Descendant

I project maturity, but I seek sensitivity.

You entered this existence with a practiced maturity that provides both a sense of confidence and a natural caution. As you get older, you grow into your Capricorn shoes, but your innate concern and consternation as you calculate the consequences of your actions will be with you until you take your final breath.

As you prepared for this lifetime, your chief objective was to take yourself seriously. You seek to honor and integrate the wisdom gained from a multitude of lifetimes, and use it to manifest a truly successful life. However, it is oh so easy to take on the burdens and responsibilities of others. When you do, the gods and cosmos force you to face the fact that your primary obligation is to yourself.

On the other hand, you didn't sign up for a life of toil, with no respite. Cancer's gen-tle sensitivity softens your heart and awakens you to a deeper dimension of your own soul. Your partners infuse you with the desire to dive deep into your inner instincts. It is in that sea of sensitivity that you can lose your way and take on the obligations of others. So you must learn to use Cancer's awareness to discover and tend to your own needs and then tend to the others in your life.

Aquarius Ascendant/Leo Descendant

I project intelligence, but I seek enthusiasm.

You breeze into life like a breath of fresh air. Your natural interest in others and quirky intelligence combine for a friendly, seemingly approachable persona, at least from a distance. If anyone gets too close, you get prickly and persnickety, certain that intimacy will dull your intellect.

Your bright idea for this lifetime is to maintain a certain level of independence and clarity as you look out at the big picture of your life. Sounds good, until you realize that in this vacuum of objectivity, you quickly become so irreverent and unpredictable that no one knows what to make of you, least of all you. So, your karmic lessons lead you back to the crucial understanding that you were not meant to be some whacko hermit. Instead, you are to maintain your autonomy within the fabric and framework of society.

Leo can entice you out of your ivory tower like no other sign and warms you from your soul to your toes. Leo reminds you that life is much more than theories scratched out on a chalkboard or the back of your hand. On the other hand, you can quickly burn out in Leo's exuberant land of experience and enchantment, so you'll do well to follow your instinct to keep your distance and keep your sanity.

Pisces Ascendant/Virgo Descendant

I project compassion, but I seek stability.

Tender and gentle, you look at life in terms of potential and possibilities fueled by magical thinking and mystical insights. Armed with instinct and inklings that are uncannily accurate when it comes to your pals, you are somehow unable to comprehend the cosmic cues and clues that could unlock unlimited possibilities in your own life. Even so, you are romantic at heart, hoping and praying for heaven on earth.

Sensitive to even the most suspect of sad sob stories, your soul's mission in this lifetime is to use that same tenderness and gentleness with yourself, and to actually listen to the still small voice that holds the clues to your destiny. Of course, it's much more fun to flirt and flounce and float along. Even then, you'll drift back around to the fundamental truth that your clairvoyance is not just a parlor trick; it's there to light your way as well as enlighten others.

On the other hand, you are not meant to be zoned out in some kind of psychotropic stupor, hoping for a glimpse beyond the veil. Virgo brings you back to earth and grounds you, providing the method and means to actually get the bills paid before the lights are shut off. While all that order and organization is a secret turn-on for you, the heavens have a fairy-tale ending in store in which you create a rock-solid reality where you really can make what you believe.

The Midheaven/IC

The sign on your tenth-house cusp, or Midheaven, describes your idea of success. It's your soul's worldly purpose and intent this time around. The qualities of the sign on the Midheaven are not things that come easy to you. To accomplish your soul's objective in this part of your chart, you'll need to extend your reach and move outside your comfort zone. By the way, the Midheaven is abbreviated as MC. In this case, MC is Latin for *Medium Coeli*, which means zenith or high point. When you think about the tenth-house cusp/MC/Midheaven, remember to keep your eye on the prize.

Conversely, the IC, also known as the *Imum Coeli*, is the lowest point in your chart. It is exactly opposite your Midheaven and is usually the same as the fourth-house cusp. It serves as the foundation for your life. When you set out to make something of yourself, you must balance the Midheaven's need to achieve with the security consciousness of the *Imum Coeli*.

As you become more familiar with astrology, you'll come to appreciate its patterns and symmetry. For example, if you have Aries on the fourth-house cusp, you automatically have Libra on the tenth-house cusp.

Aries Midheaven/Libra IC

Through action and courage, I achieve peace and harmony.

With Aries in this position, your life is founded on action and aspirations, guts and glory. At the root of every experience in your life is the need to reach deep down into that part of you that is courageous and audacious. This combination provides a healthy urge of get-up-and-go as well as some serious impatience.

In past lives, this bravado and boldness marched through your personal history. Now that you are constantly striving to define harmony and find peace, you long for the clarity of the battlefield, where the good guys were easy to recognize and everyone was working with the same strategy.

One of the great challenges of this lifetime is the temptation to give in and give up in order to escape the labyrinth of liaisons that Libra holds. However, your contract with the cosmos clearly states that you must honor the sacred flame of self-awareness that serves as the foundation for all that follows in your life.

Taurus Midheaven/Scorpio IC

Through perseverance and resolve, I achieve a sense of control and personal power.

With Taurus in this position, your life is founded on the ability to create a rock-solid sense of stability. At the root of every experience in your life is the need to have and to hold, whether we're talking about folks or fine things. Taurus in this position provides a benchmark of consistency and obstinacy unparalleled by any other sign in the zodiac.

In past lives, this steadiness and stubbornness progressed through your personal history to the point that now your solidarity is second nature. However, Scorpio reminds you that your own dogged plodding has gotten you stuck in the mud and that in order to regain control you must reach out and accept a helping hand. Surrender to the idea that you're not in this alone and that others can actually help you along the way.

One of the great challenges of this lifetime is the temptation to greedily take over the world, or at least be master of your own little corner of the universe. However, your contract with the cosmos clearly states that you must integrate your innate understanding of your own worth and others' values and project a higher principle into your professional world. Finally, it's your determination and true grit that supply the foundation for all that follows in your life.

Gemini Midheaven/Sagittarius IC

Through curiosity and diversity, I achieve personal freedom.

With Gemini in this position, your life is founded on an insatiable inquisitiveness that leads you here, there, and everywhere. This restless combination suggests that you have signed up to be the gad about town and that most days you'd rather be anywhere but where you find yourself.

In past lives, information and interaction formed the bulk of your experiences. You and your mind were constantly on the move. Now that you are aiming for the distant shores of Sagittarius, you must broaden your view and set your sights higher.

One of the great challenges of this lifetime is the temptation to quell your curious mind and project the misleading mirage that you already know everything about everything. Even so, there's no stopping the queries and quandaries that constantly stream through your consciousness. Instead, you succeed when you honor your pact with the planets to listen to the whisperings of your inner intelligence as you explore the uncharted terrain of Sagittarius.

Cancer Midheaven/Capricorn IC

Through sensitivity and nurturing, I achieve respect and admiration

With Cancer in this position, your life is founded on the strength of emotion and your quest for tenderness and sensitivity. At the root of every experience in your life is the need to be emotionally engaged and entwined with another. As a result, your receptors are always "on," and you are forced to forge ahead despite conflicting feelings and needs.

In past lives, nurturing and nourishing others was one of the cornerstones of your existence. The sad truth is that despite your greatest efforts, you are often confronted by others' lack of sensitivity and compassion toward your own wishes. In this lifetime, you must pit your needs against your hard-won wisdom that in order to feel truly secure, you must care for yourself and then open up to others' needs.

One of the great challenges of this lifetime is the temptation to bury your emotions under a rock and allow yourself to become cold and calculating. While a life devoid of aching need may seem like a safe haven, your contract with the cosmos clearly states that you must honor the emotional sensitivity that serves as your foundation while integrating the solidarity and wisdom of Capricorn.

Leo Midheaven/Aquarius IC

Through creativity and generosity, I achieve independence and autonomy.

With Leo in this position, your life is founded on following your heart's desire. At the root of every experience in your life is the need to inspire and imagine your next great creation. This combination provides a passionate drive to fashion freeform ideas into great works that reflect your own enthusiasm, warmth, and zeal.

In past lives, you ruled the roost, in one way or another. Don't get caught up in trying to figure out who you were. There's a reason we don't remember, and that's probably because the prime time is now. The point is to focus on the potential pitfalls you encountered and how you can set things straight. Maybe you and your ego were so intent on having things a certain way that in this lifetime you yearn for objectivity and awareness.

One of the great challenges of this lifetime is the temptation to disengage from the desires that drive you to invest heart and soul in your latest creation, be it a painting, love affair, or child. However, your pact with the planets clearly states that you must combine the vitality that has propelled you through countless lives with the intelligence and objectivity that Aquarius offers up.

Virgo Midheaven/Pisces IC

Through order and discipline, I achieve beauty and bliss.

Virgo in this position indicates that your life is founded on making a difference, whether through simplifying circumstances of daily life or by making a substantive contribution to the state of affairs. At the root of every experience in your life is the necessity to quietly and modestly dedicate yourself to a cause, be it another person, place, or philosophy.

Your capacity for service and sacrifice in past lives would astound you. While you may have had more than your fair share of lifetimes stuffed away in some sanctuary, you probably served plenty of time in positions that were productive and quite useful. In these lives, you gained your eye for detail and acquired your inner critic. After all that hard work, Pisces is now like a balm to your soul, calling to you to surrender the methods that have taken lifetimes to perfect.

One of the great challenges of this lifetime is the temptation to fall into the never-ending nothingness of the Pisces abyss, floating for eternity, drifting with no destiny. That's just a daydream, but your Virgo vigilance will always remind you that you must live up to the letter of the law in your celestial contract. You must stay grounded in the well-formed order and organization of Virgo while embracing the uplifting Pisces vision of heaven on earth to guide your actions and permeate your reality.

Libra Midheaven/Aries IC

Through awareness and attentiveness to others, I achieve a sense of self.

With Libra in this position, your life is founded on the constant quest for peace and equality, harmony and fairness. At the root of every experience in your life is the need to weigh and balance, adjust and acquiesce, in the pursuit of absolute correspondence and connection with another person. Fortunately, Aries' direct and straightforward nature reminds you to get to the point and make a decision, even if it isn't perfect.

In past lives, partnerships took precedence. From this experience you can extract an innate charm and capacity to make anyone your confidant. However, this ability to form affiliations based on faking it has taken its toll, and your spirit longs for the ability to just be yourself.

As you strive to reintroduce your identity into relationships, one of the great challenges of this lifetime is to have patience, both with yourself and with those you draw to you. Aries is always ready to roll, and in your quest for connection, you could go too far, too fast, and crash and burn. Instead, your rules of engagement clearly state that you must respect the lovely and loving side of Libra as a scale that constantly weighs your actions and intentions as you navigate through life.

Scorpio Midheaven/Taurus IC

Through intensity and introspection, I achieve security and stability.

With Scorpio in this position, your life is founded on the need for deep and meaningful experience. At the root of every experience is the requirement to transform and transcend the powerful forces at work in your life, yet your soul hungers for the predictable peace and quiet, security and stability, of Taurus.

Your past lives were filled with life-changing, hair-raising experiences, complete with deep, dark conspiracies, the use and misuse of power, and powerful shifts in consciousness. In other words, you weren't playing in the kiddie pool. Now, you're ready for some relaxation and reprieve from all the trauma and drama. In this lifetime, your innate ability to play with the powerful and influential constantly draws you into plots and schemes that force you to confront your own shadow and decide how you will wield your power this time around.

One of the great challenges of this lifetime is the temptation to play it safe and hide out till the trouble is over. While that might really feel like what you are searching for, the truth is that your contract with the cosmos maintains that you must indeed draw on your inner instincts and own your own power as you steer your way into the peaceful promised land of Taurus.

Sagittarius Midheaven/Gemini IC

Through exuberance and passion, I realize a multitude of options.

With Sagittarius in this position, your life is founded on the quest for knowledge, both of the world and of yourself. At the root of every experience in your life is the need to expand your consciousness and explore your world. Gemini offsets the straightforward focus of Sagittarius with simple but stimulating questions and quandaries.

You have built a travel journal of past lives in which your experiences and expressions ran the gamut of possibilities. Yet you came into this lifetime fully expectant that there was something more to discover and discuss.

One of the great challenges of this lifetime is the temptation to try to do it all, all right now. Gemini's unstructured agenda can have you flitting and flopping, darting and eventually dropping dead in your tracks, having never really gotten anywhere. The uncomplicated answer is to integrate your ability to see the big picture with Gemini's desire to stop and smell the roses, one by one, and build your success on your philosophy that the journey of a thousand miles really does begin with one single step, right in your own neighborhood.

Capricorn Midheaven/Cancer IC

Through duty and responsibility, I realize emotional security.

With Capricorn in this position, your life is founded on the wise use of power and responsibility in order to manifest success—not a short order in any lifetime. At the root of every experience in your life is the compulsion to do the right thing, and Cancer's influence allows you to integrate the emotional with the practical when it comes to making the right choices.

Chances are you've had plenty of lifetimes where you were defined by your successful or not-so-successful handling of your duties. In some ways, you may have made your career and professional responsibilities your primary focus to the detriment of your family, friends, health, or even your own soul's progression. Now, because of Cancer's prominent position in your life, you must consult your emotions as you construct your definition of success.

One of the great challenges of this lifetime is the temptation to succumb to the cries of your long-neglected inner child and immerse yourself and everyone around you in a tidal wave of feelings and needs. Fortunately, your clarity and wisdom guide you to integrate the emotional with the practiced maturity that you have polished to perfection in past lives and help you attain an authentic sense of success that honors your needs and still feathers your nest.

Aquarius Midheaven/Leo IC

Through objectivity and altruism, I achieve a generous reputation.

With Aquarius in this position, your life is founded on independence and individuality. At the root of every experience in your life is the innate need to do your own thing and to break out of old, uncreative patterns. This combination provides amazing insight and understanding into your own motives and mission in life.

In past lives, expecting the unexpected was the creed you lived by. Quite often, political situations and events beyond your control affected your identity to the point that you lost sight of your true nature. However, in this life, you are seeking a sense of the personal through Leo and are striving to project your authentic self, independent of outside influences.

One of the great challenges of this lifetime is the temptation to assume a persona and strike a pose, waiting for others to validate your sense of self. However, your Aquarian roots contrast starkly with your attempts at vanity. Your pact with the planets clearly states that you must honor the objectivity and awareness of Aquarius as you fervently pursue the passion and self-confidence of Leo.

Pisces Midheaven/Virgo IC

Through surrender and sensitivity, I achieve a sense of order.

With Pisces in this position, your life is founded on the fuzzy, formless world of inkling and intuition. Every experience in your life is based on the need to perceive, to explore your sixth sense and make sense of the cues and clues that the cosmos sends your way. Combined with Virgo, you have a potent mix of sense and sensitivity.

Your past lives reflect a timeless dedication to service and sacrifice. Your ability to extricate your spirit from your ego has allowed you to surrender to the highest heights of sacred understanding. Having spent lifetimes meditating on the meaning of life, without ever experiencing a life of your own, you have finally decided to be present in the here and now.

One of the great challenges of this lifetime is the temptation to move through the mundane and focus only on the physical. Instead, you must blend the gentle flow of Pisces with the precision of Virgo in a cosmic dance that allows you to honor the spiritual and psychic as you seek a way to put divine right order into your days.

Part One Summary

When you set out on any adventure, it's a good idea to know a bit about where you're headed and what to do once you get there. Before you take another step, make note of the insights you've gained in this section on prenatal eclipses and the compass in your chart. Here's a handy worksheet to help you keep track of it all.

If you haven't already done so, make sure to use the CD-ROM included with this book to create your own chart. It's your passport to explore your own soul's purpose. As you refer to each part of your chart, you'll notice that each description in the previous chapters begins with a cosmic clue that you can use to personalize each leg of your journey.

To use this worksheet, first make note of the sign and house positions of your prenatal eclipses. Remember those little one-liners at the beginning of each description? This is the perfect place to jot them down, along with any of your own insights. For example, let's say you were born on December 24, 1955. By using either appendix 1 or the CD-ROM program, you discover that your prenatal Solar Eclipse is in Sagittarius. Next, take a look at the section "Prenatal Solar Eclipse in Sagittarius or in the Ninth House" in chapter 1. It says that you're really here to explore your world and inspire others to do so as well. That's what you would write in the first section of the worksheet.

Let's say that your prenatal Solar Eclipse in Sagittarius falls in your tenth house. Take a look at the section "Prenatal Solar Eclipse in Capricorn or in the Tenth House" in chapter 1, which says that this placement is all about ambition, achievement, career, and climbing the corporate ladder. How do you put the sign and house placements of your prenatal eclipse together? Remember, the sign = how, the house = where. So, you are here to teach others to explore their world, and you do this primarily through your reputation or professional life.

Make note of the one-liners from these two different paragraphs in the "cosmic clue" part of the worksheet: "I teach exploration" and "I teach responsibility." This may sound a bit complex and complicated to most folks, but if it's your personal combo, it will make perfect sense to you.

At this point you'll want to make note of how all this astrological stuff relates to real-life situations and circumstance. Once you've completed the section for the prenatal Solar Eclipse, you'll want to move on to the section for the prenatal Lunar Eclipse, using the same tools and techniques. Then do the same for your Ascendant/Descendant and Midheaven/IC.

1. Prenatal Eclipses.
   - Refer to the eclipses tables in appendix 1 to determine the Solar and Lunar Eclipses that occurred prior to your birth, and note the sign of each one below.
   - My prenatal Solar Eclipse: what I'm here to teach others and the nature of my relationships.

     Sign: the principle that I am to teach others: _____

     _____

     _____

     Cosmic clue: _____

     House: the area of life in which I teach others: _____

     _____

     _____

     Cosmic clue: _____

     My own experiences: _____

     _____

     _____

   - My prenatal Lunar Eclipse: what I'm here to learn and the type of individuals I attract.

     Sign: the principle that I am here to learn: _____

     _____

     _____

     Cosmic clue: _____

House: the area of life in which I need to apply my lessons: _____

_____

_____

Cosmic clue: _____

My own experiences: _____

_____

_____

2. True north: the compass in my chart.

• My Ascendant/Descendant: how I rise up to meet life on my own, and how I approach my relationships with others.

Signs: _____

_____

_____

Cosmic clue: _____

My own experiences: _____

_____

_____

• My Midheaven/IC: what I base my actions on, and what I hope to accomplish in this lifetime.

Signs: _____

_____

_____

Cosmic clue: _____

My own experiences: _____

_____

_____

Part Two
Traveling Companions

You have places to go and people to see, so before you take another step, take a good, hard look at who is accompanying you on your journey. Don't get suckered into thinking that the other folks in your life don't affect you and your progress. The cosmic truth is that your friends and lovers either support or undermine your spiritual evolution. Just like a train ride, some folks touch your life for mere moments, while others stick around long enough to change your destiny.

The nifty thing about astrology is its capacity to describe your relationships, good or otherwise. Your chart provides ample information about your pals and partners, as well as your associates and even your enemies.

Before you read through the next few chapters, take a moment to check your chart for these points:

- *The Sun:* your passport to rise and shine; the true you in relationships.
- *The Moon:* the instincts that propel you along your path; your emotional bonds with others.
- *Conjunctions and oppositions:* the associations between planets that affect your connections with others.

Your Sun sign reflects your heart's desire, in and out of relationships. When you were mapping out your objectives for this lifetime, your Sun sign showed the best and brightest way to get there. As far as relationships go, you can never really hide who you are, so it's only fitting that the brightest body in our solar system reflects the true you.

Your Moon sign represents what you really need in order to be all that you can be. Just like the actual Sun and Moon, no matter what sign your Moon is in, it constantly reflects your Sun's own light. It reflects your needs and what it takes for you to feel good and satisfied in this lifetime. As far as relationships go, the Moon defines and describes your emotional style, the challenges you encounter in terms of getting your needs met, and what you must do to overcome these apparent obstacles. Study the signs of your Sun and Moon carefully, as their combination reflects a special mix of energy that adds up to spiritual success.

In this section, you'll also be introduced to two aspects. Remember that aspects are simply dialogue between the players in your chart. Think of them as cosmic conversations. The first and most potent aspect is the conjunction, which is another way of saying that the energy of one planet blends with another planet. Just like a dinner party, some planets do well when they are next to each other, and other planets get downright grumpy when seated next to their nemesis.

The second aspect is the opposition. Just as it sounds, this connection between planets suggests some kind of confrontation, like the shootout at the O.K. Corral. At the very least, an opposition makes you aware of two very different parts of your nature.

Conjunctions and oppositions identify key issues that affect your relationships, since relationships boil down to focusing on the issues that affect the relationship and becoming aware of who you are as well as who your partner is. Just remember that you can either work with or against the aspects in your chart.

Of course, all of this information will help you better understand your own relationship recipe that much better. Plus, it will assist you in appreciating the needs and expectations that others bring to the table. Either way, now is the perfect time to check your chart and figure out the promise and problems in your relationships.

4
Your Sun
Go with the Glow

The Sun is the source energy you use to define and refine your soul in this lifetime. Your Sun sign represents the key experience you are seeking to integrate into your soul's code. However, since most of this soul work plays out in the labyrinth of relationships, understanding your own Sun sign will help you understand your karmic intention that much better. In terms of traveling companions and karmic connections, the Sun spotlights the masculine side of your own soul, as well as your relationships with men.

Sun in Aries or in the First House

I use courage and valor to define myself.

You were born to take charge of your life, your heart, and your soul, and as a result, your relationships are based on asserting yourself. Sometimes there is a mighty fine line between asserting yourself and being downright aggressive. The point is to make your claim and still honor the good and the god in your partner. If you are female, you just love it when your guy takes charge—but not to the point that he overshadows you. If you are male, you love to play the role of conquering hero and save the damsel in distress. Either way, you can easily lose your momentum by fighting too many battles for the other guy.

As an Aries, your soul purpose is to define yourself. This is not exactly a short order, but the cosmic crew consistently helps you out by tempting you with the adventure of rushing headlong into the great unknown. While this life plan sounds impractical to your cautious Capricorn friends, it's just what the doctor ordered to help you overcome your past-life mistakes, take charge of your gifts and talents in this lifetime, and get out of your own way.

The heart and soul of every Aries are cut from the fabric of courage and nobility. That's why you look so good in uniform. Sure, you love to be loved, but the real thrill in life is to charge off to conquer the dragons that dare cross your path. But your "fight now, ask questions later" approach does find you jousting with the occasional windmill.

Libra is your opposite sign and points out the need for peace and tranquility. Use Libra's poise to grace your actions with logic and finesse. If you're not quite sure what your marching orders are, it's Libra's indecision that is causing you to wander and waffle. It's up to you to triumph over those inner demons that subconsciously make you timid and tentative.

The key to tending the sacred Aries flame is to embrace your true-blue nature and circle your soul with courage. Be willing to risk, to break new ground, to make a path for others to follow. Reach for the biggest, the brightest, and the best without reservation or apology, and then you will indeed embody the spirit of the conquering hero of your soul.

Sun in Taurus or in the Second House

I employ steadiness and perseverance to define myself.

Nickels, dimes, dollars, and diamonds: how do you measure up? You were born a Taurus to do one thing: to discover the value of yourself and everything around you. Deep down is the need to have and to hold, to pursue and possess all for the sake of feeling secure. At times, your quest for the stuff of stability reels out of control, when innocent wishes turn into unquenchable cravings fueled by the fear of never having enough.

Taurus has a kinder, gentler side that tempts and entices you to step away from your "make a buck" existence and commune with nature. Sit a spell, and watch the clouds go by. Breathe deep and listen as the rock-solid earth beneath you asks if your life is rich with pleasure as well as treasures.

Scorpio is your opposite sign and makes no bones about Taurus's blind ambition to have it all. You can rebalance your life by adopting Scorpio's firm belief that if having something feeds your hunger but not your soul, you should let it go and move on to greener pastures. Of course, if you stalwartly stand your ground and refuse to relinquish your possessions, you can be certain that you've been bitten by the dark side of Scorpio's obsession with power and control.

Eventually, in your own time, you happen upon the greatest prize of all: the reality that the purpose of life isn't just about having for the sake of having. Once you embrace this cosmic truth, your strength and tenacity propel you forward on an unstoppable quest to have the right stuff, the stuff that matters, and the stuff of which dreams are made.

Sun in Gemini or in the Third House

I draw on curiosity and flexibility to define myself.

As a Gemini, your soul purpose is to delight in the ever changing options and opportunities, choices and chances, that await you on life's highways and byways. Instead of trying to plant your feet and pin down the secret to success, awaken your Gemini soul with a quick trip into the curious land of "what if?" What if you didn't have to work full-time? What if you finished that book you started to write when you were in college? What if you lived on the beach for a year? What if you really could have your cake and eat it too?

Sagittarius is your opposite sign and urges you to expand your mind and explore the big, wide world. Of course, those are both noble pursuits, but if you find yourself stalled in search of the meaning of it all, you can rest assured you've been poisoned by Sagittarius's pompous philosophy that everything has to make sense. You don't need to buy into that singular view of life. As a Gemini, you can make peace with the fact that your life is like a day trip into the land of enigmas, paradoxes, and oxymorons. Actually, that's a good thing.

Allow yourself to wonder and wander, pause and ponder, as the world of possibilities dances in front of you. As you hop, skip, and jump through the kaleidoscopic landscape that your soul calls home, embrace Gemini's clever capacity to refresh your psyche with interesting insights and even more interesting questions. If you expect to emerge from your time on the Gemini clock with the meaning of life, you'll be sorely disappointed. The Gemini twins giggle at the naïve simplicity of the idea and hint that in asking the what-if questions, you have already started on a journey that is much more important than simply finding the answer.

Sun in Cancer or in the Fourth House

I draw on emotional sensitivity to define myself.

As a Cancer, your soul purpose is to put down some roots and surround yourself with loved ones. Learn to go with the flow of your softer, sensitive side and open up to your inner voice. Hone your instincts, and act on your gut feelings. While you don't need to take on house and home with the fervor of Martha Stewart, a few domestic talents will serve you well, especially in the wee hours of the morning when your best friend shows up on your doorstep to cry on your shoulder. That's when brewing a comforting cup of tea can make all the difference.

Of course, Cancer is not all about sugarplums and soccer moms. As a Cancer, you can apply your sensitivity and limitless imagination to almost anything you choose. What's the catch? Simply that you have to be in the right mood to do much of anything, so your life's work had better be something that makes you happy. Otherwise, throughout your career, you'll find yourself sidestepping responsibility and being labeled as cranky, cantankerous, and ornery.

Cool, emotionally remote Capricorn is your opposite and goads you into setting the occasional boundary so that your friends and family respect you. The minute your mood swings over toward cold and calculating, you know you've ventured too far into the cut-and-dried world of Capricorn. Then you know it's time to return to the gentle ebb and flow of emotions and intuition.

Since you have chosen to experience life through the lens of sentiment and sensitivity, you simply need to claim the power inherent in your compassionate nature. Use your emotion as a touchstone, a helpful guide to navigating through the maze of family and feelings, heart and soul.

Sun in Leo or in the Fifth House

I use creativity and generosity to define myself.

Born into the lusty sign of Leo, your soul purpose is to pursue passion's promise in all you do, whether it's writing the great American novel or creating a special rendezvous with your dream lover. Leo demands that you put your heart into every aspect of your existence and that you create a life to be proud of.

Your charismatic warmth and generous spirit easily make you the center of attention. Deep down, you love holding court and displaying your finer points in front of an adoring audience, but it's up to you what you do with all that popularity. In the land of Leo, either your ego can swell with plenty of pretentious self-importance, or you can plow past your pride and access that part of you that is capable of noble humility, leadership, and ingenuity.

Aquarius is your opposite sign and offers a cool, breezy objectivity to offset your fiery passions. Use Aquarius's fascination for the future to define your goals and plans for the next week, month, and year. However, when you find yourself feeling cut off from the excitement of everyday life, then you have indeed taken a detour into Aquarius's penchant to disengage when things get too dicey. Remember that as a Leo, you thrive on the chaos of creation, so it's up to you to revive your life with inspiration and innovation.

As a Leo, your spirit reminds you that this lifetime is not a dress rehearsal. Rather, it is about mastering your self-expression so that you exude confidence and graciousness and inspire respect and loyalty. In order for your soul to take center stage, you must honor the irrepressible enthusiasm that inflames your imagination and commands your inner light to shine.

Sun in Virgo or in the Sixth House

I draw on a gentle practicality to define myself.

Being born a Virgo presents you with the perfect opportunity to create your own little island of perfection. It is your chance to order your world according to your vision. You must balance the fight for flawlessness with real-world practicality. Avoid obsession with trivial tasks, and choose instead to dedicate your efforts toward making a difference.

Sure, anyone can talk big, but as a Virgo, you actually follow up on those big words with even bigger actions and accomplishments. Virgo just loves the feeling that comes from a job well done and the sense of satisfaction that comes from creating order out of chaos. Of course, the devil is in the details, but it's up to you to recognize that sometimes a bit of bedlam is actually part of divine right order. Otherwise, you'll live up to your fusspot, finicky reputation.

Dreamy Pisces is your opposite sign. You may scoff at Pisces' hopeful faith and innate idealism, pointing out that it's actually hard work that gets things done. However, a day trip to the enchanted land of Pisces every once in a while is a salve to your soul. Use Pisces' compassion and acceptance to acknowledge your strengths and imperfections. Just be wary of drifting along under the spell of Pisces for too long, or you'll find it harder and harder to deal with the real world.

It is your wholesome, helpful nature that is a gift to others, and it is crucial to acknowledge that your passionate devotion results in important contributions to the world around you. Take pride in your striving and make peace with your inner critic, realizing that it is this capacity to discern and distinguish that your soul longs to perfect in this lifetime.

Sun in Libra or in the Seventh House

I draw on grace and charm to define myself.

According to the travel brochure from the lush land of Libra, you're nobody unless you book passage on the ship of dreams with your one and only. Yes, you are here to understand your relationship to the world and everyone in it. You typically bend over backwards to force yourself to match your beloved's worldview rather than accepting the differences between the two of you. Not surprisingly, finding or becoming the perfect partner is not your soul purpose. Preserving your individuality and seeking harmony and peace without sacrificing yourself is what your soul truly craves.

Once your illusions have been blasted to bits, it's easy to find refuge in Libra's second-favorite pastime of weighing the pros and cons of every issue before pronouncing judgment. Unfortunately, you won't see that life is passing you by while you mull over the rhetorical and the theoretical.

Your opposite sign is Aries, which gives you the occasional kick in the seat of the pants and insists that you do something, even if it's wrong. Your Aries shadow can turn love into a battlefield and create a mindset of confrontation and contention in even the most casual of interactions. The minute you tackle the convenience-store clerk because she didn't smile at you is the time you need to take a deep breath, relax, and resume your quest for peace and tranquility in Libra.

You've been blessed with natural charm and grace as much to enhance your own being as to attract romantic relationships. As you move through life, use Libra's unerring scales to balance your life and to make sure that your wants and needs are part of the equation. If you decide to walk arm in arm with someone who honors you every step of the way, well, the heavens above couldn't be happier.

Sun in Scorpio or in the Eighth House

I draw on intensity and passion to define myself.

On a soul level, you have chosen this lifetime to master the deep, driving desire to create a longer, stronger link with the power that controls the cosmos. But first you have to exorcise the ghosts and goblins that haunt your soul and convert the monsters of your mind into powerful allies.

The dynamic, resourceful power that flows through you can single-handedly work miracles, and you are quite familiar with chaos and upheaval as the messy but necessary processes of transformation. However, to truly become master and commander of your capacity to help and heal, you must hone your instincts and ability to read others' motives and emotions.

Your opposite sign is stable, secure Taurus. Lounging around Taurus's lush, plush pasturelands provides some much-needed peace and tranquility in which you can relax and release the resentments and obsessions that clutter your mind. In addition, Taurus can help you take stock of your possessions and grace your life with gratitude. Unfortunately, it's ever so easy to get stuck in the Taurus mud and spin your wheels, mistaking action for progress. Ultimately, it's up to you to extract yourself from the crushing comforts of Taurus and pursue the passions and perils of Scorpio's depths.

Claim your place as the most powerful sign of the zodiac. Make peace with the fact that the power streaming through you can either empower or destroy whomever and whatever you hold near and dear. At the end of the day, it is this intimate awareness of life's sacred process that ultimately liberates your soul and sets the stage for an authentic life.

Sun in Sagittarius or in the Ninth House

I use the search for freedom to define myself.

Bigger, better, faster, stronger. In this lifetime, your optimistic soul has ventured into the "everything and more" store of Sagittarius. Somewhere along the pursuit of plenty, your Sagittarian soul must answer two revealing questions: how much is enough, and how far are you willing to go to get it? Of course, as a Sagittarius, you can overextend yourself and your resources with the best of them, but eventually you end up at the same truth that freedom-loving Sagittarius has been preaching for eons: you are a spiritual nomad, so travel like one. Stop looking to fill yourself up with baubles and trinkets from the same old stores when your soul is craving the action, adventure, and the exhilaration that only comes from beginning a new journey.

Your opposite sign is options-oriented Gemini. It's never a bad idea to make a quick pit stop at the Gemini garage before setting off toward parts unknown. Inform yourself, investigate your options, and make a few phone calls to let people know when and where you are headed. But don't tarry. Once you've decided on your course, stick with it. Otherwise, Gemini's excessive array of alternatives will overwhelm your mind and scatter your intentions to the four winds. If you find yourself buzzing around in circles, you need to pull out your compass and focus on traveling in one direction, one step at a time.

The secret to your soul's satisfaction is to recognize that the purpose behind your wild exploits is to expand your understanding of who you are and who you are becoming. Be daring and bold, and jump headlong into the great adventures that await you. Just remember to thank your lucky stars every night, no matter where you land.

Sun in Capricorn or in the Tenth House

I use the desire to achieve and accomplish to define myself.

As a Capricorn, your soul purpose is to take yourself seriously and to honor your own wisdom. You have a disciplined drive and ambition and easily take on additional responsibilities. Your innate efficiency can be a great boon to any project or organization, but it is just as important to ensure that your hard work pays off in your own life. Organize your efforts so that you benefit as much as the next guy, and create a solid plan for success.

While your flashy Leo friends may call you a stick-in-the-mud, your patient perseverance pays off in the long run. Your reserved nature masks a powerhouse of industrious innovation that is capable of founding and following through on massive projects.

Shy, sensitive Cancer is your opposite sign. Incorporating Cancer's empathy deepens your understanding of human nature and needs. Your innate patience and wisdom can benefit your projects as well as others', but you must be cautious of being used by those who play on your fears. Draw upon your natural practicality to create appropriate boundaries to guide your personal and professional relationships.

As you march through life, conquering one project at a time, remember that life is not just about accomplishment. Make every day count, whether you meet with success or failure. Inwardly, you will always keep an eye on the prize, but you must make time for what matters. Embrace the pragmatic philosophy of wise, old Capricorn to face your fears, listen to your inner wisdom, do something worthwhile, and take personal responsibility for manifesting your dreams.

Sun in Aquarius or in the Eleventh House

I draw on the quest for individuality to define myself.

The cosmic wake-up call for your Aquarian soul is to reinvent yourself and to accept and expect the unexpected. You are rattled, restless, and ravenous for change, not just in your own life but in the lives of those around you. You're concerned with the future and fixed on the idea of grooving to the beat of a distant drummer. Draw on your inner confidence and conviction, and talk about who you really are, what you want, and your quirky ideas about the future, despite the fact that the future is always unshaped and uncertain, dicey and downright dangerous. But, that's the ultimate power of the unknown.

Aquarius requires two things to work its radical wonders: space in which to spread out and a room with a view. Get away from it all, and stand back and peer at your life project from a different angle. Be impartial. Acknowledge what arouses your passions and motivates you to move toward your dreams.

Your opposite sign is proud, rowdy Leo. Use Leo's warmth to infuse your ideas and inventions with a magnetic zeal that inspires others to contribute to your cause. Unfortunately, Leo's ego and pride can eclipse your idealistic and unaffected nature. Listen to your inner voice, and free yourself from the quicksand of self-importance.

It is an enigma that the same altruistic attitude that inspires you to dream also peppers your life with surprising twists and turns, dead ends and detours. When the unexpected strikes, take a moment to gather your thoughts and redesign your strategy. Then, hold fast to the undeniable truth that when you keep on keeping on, when you hold the dream, your soul can truly be alive and liberated, now and in the future.

Sun in Pisces or in the Twelfth House

I draw on my inner vision to define myself.

As you thread your way through the labyrinth of life, your soul purpose is to honor your intuition and have faith in the power of your dreams. Your tender soul seeks tranquility, and yet your desire to help, serve, and sacrifice constantly draws you into the deep uncharted waters of personal relationships. It is there that your romantic nature seeks to combine with the divine as you navigate love's mists and myths in search of heaven on earth.

As a Pisces, you have an unshakeable faith and can peer into the pitch-black abyss of human nature, knowing that there is an undeniable goodness at the heart of every soul. Your compassion and accepting nature enable you to connect with anyone and everyone, but no matter how poorly you are treated in response, your core beliefs are never tarnished. Even so, you must learn to grieve and mourn. You may have plenty of delays and disappointments, regrets and lamentations, but becoming a martyr simply robs you of your divinity.

Because you see the world as it could be, as it should be, you are an artist at heart. Give play to your imagination, and allow your creative forces a free hand. The results will be a fascinating combination of realism and fantasy, whimsy and myth.

Vigilant Virgo is your opposite sign and offers a helping hand in terms of organizing your life and staying on track. Gentle Virgo guides you through the practical considerations of everyday tasks. Virgo's unrelenting focus on form will eventually debilitate your dreams and visions. Instead, give in to your Pisces muse who woos you to relax and go with the flow, to succumb to a little bit of fantasy, and to resolve and relinquish the regrets and misgivings that litter your subconscious.

Finally, you must surrender to your inner light and listen to the silent whispers of the cosmos. Look inside and see not what you are, but what you can be when you trust that you are exactly where you are meant to be, right here, right now.

5
Your Moon
Lighting Your Path

While your Sun takes center stage and lets your personality shine through, your Moon is happy as a clam to work in the background, running the show from behind the scenes. If you need an example of how your needs run the show, think of a crying baby in a restaurant. No matter what you do to try to tune out the baby's cries, you won't enjoy your dinner until someone takes care of the baby.

The simple truth is that your needs must be honored, or your life will become one disappointing experience after another. The good news about the Moon's role in your life is that it puts you in charge of meeting your own needs. In other words, you don't have to wait for some Prince or Princess Charming to ride in and rescue you.

It's easy to project your karmic responsibility to meet your own needs onto another person and fall prey to the notion that the other person is your path to pleasure. Of course, there's nothing like a loving relationship to make your day, but the minute you believe that another person holds the key to your happiness, you imprison yourself and your needs behind bars.

As you read through the information on your Moon sign, make note of the things you can do to make your own life better and comfort yourself. The bonus to this is that as you acknowledge and act on your own needs, you'll attract others who are doing the same.

Moon in Aries or in the First House

I need to act on my feelings and instincts.

At the time of your birth, the Moon was charging through Aries with all the impatient abandon of a two-year-old bent on having first dibs in the sandbox. As a result, your own emotional interactions are flavored by an innocence and energy not found in any other part of the zodiac.

In past lives you were the conquering hero, focused on fighting for others' rights and losing yourself in the battle for truth, justice, and all that other stuff. Now the self-oriented Aries Moon, acting as your emotional barometer, reflects your soul's goal to figure out what you really want. Your needs and desires, your emotions and instincts, all start and end with you and your emerging sense of self.

This by no means suggests that you are selfish or that you are bound to a life of oneness. In fact, your straight-shooting Aries Moon is a big selling point in the land of romance, and others are drawn to your uncomplicated approach to relationships. On the other hand, you're likely to have more than your fair share of immature, self-centered folks cross your path. Fortunately, once your trusting Aries Moon figures out you're being taken for a ride, you're out of there in no time flat.

If your Sun is also in Aries, you were born at the time of the new Moon, emphasizing a soul-deep desire to define and refine your sense of self as you move through this lifetime. If your Sun is in Libra, you were born on the full Moon and constantly seek to contrast and compare your own bravado with the apparent strengths of others.

The soul-deep desires illuminated by your Moon in Aries are strengthened by a Gemini, Leo, Sagittarius, or Aquarius Sun sign. However, the Sun in Taurus, Cancer, Virgo, Scorpio, Capricorn, or Pisces creates a desire for order and emotional stability. In this case, you are constantly challenged to blend and somehow integrate your need for passion and excitement with the enigmatic longing to create security and stability.

Moon in Taurus or in the Second House

I need to create security based on my needs and instincts.

At the time of your birth, the Moon was grounding itself in the tangible terrain of Taurus, with the well-defined mission to learn to stand your ground. In light of this, your emotional dealings with others are affected by the search for stability and the quest for permanence.

In past lives, you were solid as a rock, always there, come rain or come shine, as others danced in and out of your heart. Unfortunately, you found yourself alone on the dance floor one too many times. Even so, your emotions and instincts propel you forward in a steadfast pursuit of your one and only who will always be there for you. Your Taurus Moon, serving as your emotional compass, directs you to have and to hold on for dear life.

This by no means suggests that you are innately possessive or controlling. On the other hand, you're likely to have more than your fair share of domineering folks who masquerade as loving partners who supposedly know what's best for you. Regardless, you must return to your home turf and center yourself in the solidarity of your soul.

If your Sun is also in Taurus, you were born at the time of the new Moon, emphasizing a desire to develop a strong sense of self-worth and values as you move through this lifetime. If your Sun is in Scorpio, you were born near the full Moon and constantly seek to contrast and compare your own resolve with the apparent willpower of others.

The soul-deep desires illuminated by your Moon in Taurus are strengthened by a Cancer, Virgo, Capricorn, or Pisces Sun sign. However, the Sun in Aries, Gemini, Leo, Libra, Sagittarius, or Aquarius impassions you with a driving desire for new and varied experiences. In this case, you are constantly challenged to blend and somehow integrate your need for constancy with your secret hunger for excitement.

Moon in Gemini or in the Third House

I need to communicate my needs and instincts.

At the time of your birth, the Moon was dancing through Gemini's land of options and opportunities with all the joyful anticipation of a kid in a candy store. This childlike approach to life's choices adds a never-ending variety to your partners and partnerships as you move along life's path.

You were everyone's sounding board in past lives. There simply wasn't anything others couldn't tell you. Sadly, those same folks who benefited from your emotional resiliency and objectivity never stopped to ask about your life and times. Now the Gemini Moon, acting as your emotional indicator, helps you move from relationship to relationship in the single-minded desire to be heard and to give voice to your deepest feelings and fears.

This by no means suggests you are fickle or flaky. On the other hand, you're likely to attract plenty of flighty partners, and their lack of kindness and consideration compels you to act as if it's no skin off your teeth. Eventually, your Gemini Moon will have its say, and there's no time like the present to start talking about your needs.

If your Sun is also in Gemini, you were born at the time of the new Moon, emphasizing a desire to identify and voice your feelings as you move through this lifetime. If your Sun is in Sagittarius, you were born on the full Moon and constantly seek to contrast and compare your own ideas with the apparent inspiration of others.

The soul-deep desires illuminated by your Moon in Gemini are strengthened by an Aries, Leo, Libra, or Aquarius Sun sign. However, the Sun in Taurus, Cancer, Virgo, Scorpio, Capricorn, or Pisces makes you wish for roots and heritage, security and order. In this case, you are constantly challenged to blend and somehow integrate your need for experience with the enigmatic longing for substance and stability.

Moon in Cancer or in the Fourth House

I need to nurture my own needs and instincts.

At the time of your birth, the Moon was homing in on the tenderness and tranquility of hearth and home. Consequently, you are instinctively drawn to create a safe harbor for matters of the heart.

In past lives, you were the neighborhood mom, with plenty of warm cookies and gentle words of encouragement for anyone and everyone who entered your front door. Sure, that made you popular enough, but at the end of the day, there was no one to take care of you. Now the Cancer Moon illuminates your soul's goal to respond to your own needs as well as others' needs, but in that order.

This by no means suggests you are emotionally self-centered. In fact, it's easy to get thrown off balance as a parade of folks who seemingly need your ministrations whine and moan in the background of your life. Instead, you must respond to the truth that you must nurture and nourish your soul, both spiritually and physically, in this lifetime.

If your Sun is also in Cancer, you were born at the time of the new Moon, emphasizing a soul quest to flow with the emotional current as you navigate through this lifetime. If your Sun is in Capricorn, you were born on the full Moon and constantly seek to contrast and compare your own emotional needs with the apparent wisdom of others.

The soul-deep desires illuminated by your Moon in Cancer are strengthened by a Taurus, Virgo, Scorpio, or Pisces Sun sign. However, the Sun in Aries, Gemini, Libra,

Sagittarius, or Aquarius makes you long for the thrill of adventure. In this case, you must combine your need for tranquility with the part of your soul that wishes for the winds of change.

Moon in Leo or in the Fifth House

I need to be passionate about my own needs and instincts.

At the time of your birth, the Moon was stealing the show in the grand land of Leo. Your emotional style is, to say the least, warm, generous, and just a bit on the dramatic side. But then who wants to live a life of quiet desperation when you can have a lifetime of something wonderful?

In past lives, you were the ruler in your tribe, overseeing the emotional well-being of anyone and everyone, making sure they all had a chance to sing their song. Of course, that didn't leave much time or energy for love and lust, fun or frenzy. Now your plan is to have plenty of passion and pleasure, or someone is going to hear about it.

At the heart of all this drama is your quest for a soul mate who shares your lust for life without raining on your parade. This sounds simple enough on paper, but in practice it's a very different story. At the end of the day, you must go where your heart leads you and enjoy yourself every step of the way.

If your Sun is also in Leo, you were born on the new Moon, accentuating a core desire to create your life on your terms as you move through this lifetime. If your Sun is in Aquarius, you were born on the full Moon and constantly seek to contrast and compare your own freedom with the apparent independence of others.

The soul-deep desires illuminated by your Moon in Leo are strengthened by an Aries, Gemini, Libra, or Sagittarius Sun sign. However, the Sun in Taurus, Cancer, Virgo, Scorpio, Capricorn, or Pisces generates a need for stability and security. In this case, you are constantly challenged to blend and somehow integrate your craving for passion with a secret taste for permanence.

Moon in Virgo or in the Sixth House

I need to categorize my needs and instincts.

The Moon was cautiously and conscientiously crossing the Virgo threshold at the time of your birth. Ever since then, you have become aware of how important boundaries are in your search for emotional contentment.

In past lives you were quick to serve, as you dreamt of making a tangible difference in the world. Unfortunately, others may have taken advantage of your gentle and giving spirit and worked you to death—literally. Now, the Virgo Moon, acting as your emotional barometer, reflects your soul's goal to discern and determine who and what is really best for you.

Your relationships are one learning experience after another, starting and ending with your conscious declaration to carefully discriminate between your needs and others' expectations. However, the more you stick with a plan and honor the part of you that needs order, even in the midst of passion, the better your life will be.

Others might be put off by your apparently finicky nature. On the other hand, you've learned through sad experience that if you don't take charge and take a good look at who and what you're inviting into your inner sanctum, you'll end up with a big mess and an even bigger disappointment.

You were born at the time of the new Moon if your Sun is also in Virgo. This accentuates a spiritual quest to identify the delicate shifts and shades of your emotional makeup. If your Sun is in Pisces, you were born on the full Moon and constantly seek to contrast and compare the structure of your own life with the apparently effortless bliss of others' lives.

The soul-deep desires illuminated by your Moon in Virgo are strengthened by a Taurus, Cancer, Scorpio, or Capricorn Sun sign. However, the Sun in Aries, Gemini, Leo, Libra, or Sagittarius makes you wish for thrills and excitement. In that situation, you are constantly challenged to blend your innate need to express order and simplicity with the devilish desire to let loose and explore your wild and crazy side.

Moon in Libra or in the Seventh House

I need to balance my needs and instincts.

At the time of your birth, the Moon was entering the well-mannered world of Libra, and you had every intention of living a life of serenity among the politically correct and upper crust of society. That was the plan, but instead you are constantly opposed by cads who run rampant over your needs and don't even have the good grace to apologize.

In past lives, you were a great people pleaser. In fact, you may have been so good at acquiescing that folks associated you more with the peace you provided than with your true nature. Now that you're armed with a Libra Moon, you're ready to set a few things straight. If you wait for the other person to make the first move, you'll be sorely disappointed.

As you move through life, you're likely to have more than your fair share of partners who play on your need for partnership. They fake and flatter their way into your confidence only to take advantage of your never-ending sense of fair play. Ultimately, it's up to you to create peace and harmony in your life, whether you're with someone or flying solo.

If your Sun is also in Libra, you were born at the time of the new Moon, focusing on a personal aspiration to establish and maintain your equilibrium as you move through this lifetime. If your Sun is in Aries, you were born on the full Moon and constantly seek to contrast and compare your own actions with the apparent courage of others.

The soul-deep desires illuminated by your Moon in Libra are strengthened by a Gemini, Leo, Sagittarius, or Aquarian Sun sign. However, the Sun in Taurus, Cancer, Virgo, Scorpio, Capricorn, or Pisces produces a longing for protection. You are frequently tested to combine your need for experience and understanding with the enigmatic craving for peace and refuge.

Moon in Scorpio or in the Eighth House

I need to deepen my understanding of my needs and instincts.

As you entered this world, the Moon was plunging into the deep, dark, and delicious depths of Scorpio, filling you with a profound need to understand the mysteries of life and death and everything in between.

In past lives, you were on one side or the other of the power game. Either you pulled the strings and called the shots as you held the destiny of others in your hands, or you were tossed adrift on the waves of others' whims, managed and manipulated to the point that your own power became a distant and indistinct memory. The good news is that in this lifetime, you've got plenty of power, but you have to learn the fine art of control. Just like a novice firefighter with a fire hose surging and spurting at full blast, you have to learn how to direct your emotional energy without losing control, or worse yet, hurting and harming others.

Your soul's deepest desire is to have the strength and strategy to quickly move through the mundane motions of life so that you still have plenty of passion to ponder the enigmas and paradoxes, labyrinths and riddles, that lie beyond the mind-numbing actions of everyday life. In essence, your needs and desires, your emotions and instincts, all start and end with you and your craving to know the secrets of the gods and the cosmos and everything in between.

If your Sun is also in Scorpio, you were born at the time of the new Moon, accentuating a hunger to embrace your own power without diminishing another's strength. If your Sun is in Taurus, you were born on the full Moon and constantly seek to contrast and compare your own power with the apparent willfulness of others.

The soul-deep desires illuminated by your Moon in Scorpio are strengthened by a Cancer, Virgo, Capricorn, or Pisces Sun. However, the Sun in Aries, Gemini, Leo, Libra, Sagittarius, or Aquarius creates a desire for outgoing interaction. In this case, you are constantly challenged to blend and integrate your need for privacy with the enigmatic longing for contact.

Moon in Sagittarius or in the Ninth House

I need to seek out my needs and instincts.

At the time of your birth, the Moon was setting out on an adventure in the big, wide, wonderful world of Sagittarius. Consequently, you view life as one quest after another, constantly searching to expand your understanding of the world as well as your own role in it.

In past lives you inspired others to follow their own star. Meanwhile, your own mind was on fire with the passion of learning and developing a philosophy all your own. However, it's quite likely that you mistook knowledge for actual experience and rarely ventured out from the comforts of the university or the rectory where you served. Now, the Sagittarius Moon is continually infecting you with an incurable wanderlust, luring you to escape the comfortable familiarity of your locale and venture out into the great unknown. Your needs and desires, your emotions and instincts, all start and end with your longing to be anywhere but here.

If your Sun is also in Sagittarius, you were born at the time of the new Moon, implying that your soul wants to focus on actually experiencing this world, rather than gleaning what you can from dog-eared history books and coffee-stained travel brochures. If your Sun is in Gemini, you were born on the full Moon and instinctively contrast and compare your own knowledge against the information that others seem to possess.

The soul-deep desires illuminated by your Moon in Sagittarius are strengthened by an Aries, Leo, Libra, or Aquarius Sun. However, the Sun in Taurus, Cancer, Virgo, Scorpio, or Capricorn creates a desire for structure and stability. In this case, you are forever challenged to blend and integrate your need for freedom with the puzzling desire to establish roots and assume responsibility.

Moon in Capricorn or in the Tenth House

I need to be responsible for my needs and instincts.

At the time of your birth, the Moon was assuming responsibility in the conscientious command center of Capricorn. As a result, your approach to life is all business, and you take yourself, and the world around you, seriously.

In past lives, you were always the bridesmaid, never the bride. Your ability to serve and assist others in their ascent toward power was legendary. You were the power behind the throne, but rarely got the respect and admiration you deserved. Now, the Capricorn Moon, acting as your emotional barometer, reflects your soul's goal to be respected and revered without sacrificing your all-too-human need for emotional tenderness and kindness from others. In fact, your needs and desires, emotions and instincts, all start and end with your need to respect yourself and, in matters of true importance, to become your own authority.

If your Sun is also in Capricorn, you were born at the time of the new Moon, indicating that your soul's highest ambition is to achieve something substantial, both in your own life and for those around you. If your Sun is in Cancer, you were born on the full Moon, and you contrast and compare your own constitution with the seeming security of others.

The soul-deep desires illuminated by your Moon in Capricorn are strengthened by a Taurus, Virgo, Scorpio, or Pisces Sun. However, the Sun in Aries, Gemini, Leo, Libra, Sagittarius, or Aquarius instills a desire to ease your worries and enjoy the experiences along the way. In this case, you are consistently tested to balance your need for material success with the enigmatic longing to embrace the act of creation without eyeballing the bottom line or caring about the consequences.

Moon in Aquarius or in the Eleventh House

I need to act independently in terms of my needs and instincts.

The Moon was angling into the "anything goes" brainstorm of Aquarius when you were born. As a result, your ideas and emotions are forever entwined, snaking around each other like an elegant strand of DNA. Much of your life is spent in an attempt to separate your feelings from knowledge, inklings from intelligence.

In past lives, you were the logical, dispassionate friend whose advice and insight were sought in times of trouble. You could see the forest and the trees in the lives of your pals and partners, but you never quite got around to breaking out of your own ruts. That's what this lifetime is for, so your rabble-rouser Aquarian Moon is bent on the notion that now is the time to change your thinking and change your life. Just to make sure you don't get too comfortable, the roller-coaster ride of Aquarius slings you and your emotions to and fro as you hang on by the skin of your teeth. That's not to say that you won't experience calm and comfort. Don't worry—you'll have your fair share of Kodak moments. Just be aware that anytime you feel like your emotional life looks like a three-ring circus, maybe the heavens are trying to motivate you to give up your old, outmoded belief systems that have you running around in circles.

If your Sun is also in Aquarius, you were born at the time of the new Moon, highlighting a spiritual need to radically redefine yourself and the group of folks you hang out with, as you move through this lifetime. If your Sun is in Leo, you were born on the full Moon and constantly contrast and compare your own individuality with the confidence that others appear to possess.

The soul-deep desires illuminated by your Moon in Aquarius are strengthened by an Aries, Gemini, Libra, or Sagittarius Sun. However, the Sun in Taurus, Cancer, Virgo, Scorpio, Capricorn, or Pisces creates a desire for the familiar comforts of hearth and home. In this case, you are often confronted by your need for autonomy as opposed to your secret yearning for connection and community.

Moon in Pisces or in the Twelfth House

I need to be sensitive to the subtleties of my needs and instincts.

As you entered this life, the Moon retreated into Pisces' restorative and recuperative spa. As a result, you are forever searching for that same idyllic tranquility in your emotions and your family life. In reality, it's no more than a sugarplum vision spun of hopes, wishes, and dreams.

In past lives, you tended, nurtured, and cherished others until you were blue in the face—literally! Chances are you died taking care of someone or something else, all the while overlooking the most basic of your own needs. In this lifetime, you are so sensitive that you can't help but listen to your inner self as it reels off a personal to-do list that includes such simple instructions as eat your vegetables and get enough sleep. This doesn't necessarily mean that you are a natural hypochondriac, totally focused on your own signs and symptoms. Actually, you still have plenty of that tender sensitivity from lifetimes past. The point is that you have to use it to your own benefit this time around.

If your Sun is also in Pisces, you were born at the time of the new Moon, emphasizing a spiritual yearning to submerge yourself in the dreamy waters of Pisces as you move through this lifetime. If your Sun is in Virgo, you were born on the full Moon and find yourself constantly comparing your own sensitivity with the gentle understanding that others seem to possess.

The soul-deep desires illuminated by your Moon in Pisces are strengthened by a Taurus, Cancer, Scorpio, or Capricorn Sun sign. However, the Sun in Aries, Gemini, Leo, Libra, Sagittarius, or Aquarius creates a desire to initiate and instigate grand new plans. In this case, you are constantly challenged to blend and somehow integrate your need for sweet surrender on the spiritual plane with the longing to hook up with others in the here and now.

6
Conjunctions and Oppositions
Cosmic Encounters

Cosmic connections, otherwise known as aspects, between the planets offer additional information about your own inner dialogue, your relationships with the world, as well as the other souls who grace your life. Just as in life, some cosmic conversations are better than others. For instance, a loving exchange with your sweetie is a whole lot different than an ominous phone call from the IRS. Just keep that in mind, and you'll soon be a well-seasoned traveler on the aspect express. Aspects flavor the exchange between the two planets and enable you to integrate each planet into your life plan. Even so, some aspects have a bad reputation, and you'll do well to respect the positive potential as well as the destructive power inherent in any planetary conversation. Aspects, interpreted from a karmic or spiritual point of view, offer rich insights into your past lives, present conditions, and, most importantly, your soul's intentions.

As any beginning astrology student will tell you, aspects can make your eyes cross. However, if you can watch the weather report and decide whether you'll need a raincoat, you can easily figure out the aspects that occur in your own chart. All you have to do is remember that the type of conversation is defined by the nature of the aspect and the personality of the planets involved.

For example, let's say that you have Venus conjunct Mercury. A conjunction blends the nature of the two planets involved. In this case, Mercury (your desire to communicate) blends with Venus (your desire to relate). In other words, you see conversation as an important part of a relationship. On the other hand, let's say that you have Mercury conjunct Mars. Again, it's the same blending energy, but in this case it combines your desire to communicate (Mercury) with your desire to assert yourself (Mars). Chances are you're quick to get your two cents' worth into a conversation. The point is, it's the same type of aspect, but the meaning is quite different because of the planets involved.

Conjunctions: Karmic Ties That Bind

The first type of aspect is called a conjunction and occurs when two planets are right next to each other. Just like watercolors running together, conjunctions blend and blur the planets' energies together in your personality as well as your spiritual experiences and everyday activities. Conjunctions naturally emphasize the sign and the house where they are located and accentuate both the positive and negative attributes of the planets involved.

Conjunctions to the Sun

My desire to create and lead merges with the nature of the other planet.

Your personality is affected by the nature of the nearby planet. Your ability to lead, create, and be generous is either helped or hindered by the other planet, depending on how you integrate this aspect.

Conjunctions to the Moon

My desire to nurture and express my emotions merges with the nature of the other planet.

Your feelings and needs are affected by the personality of the other planet. Your ability to nurture, parent, and be sensitive to the needs of others is either helped or hindered by the other planet, depending on your awareness of these forces at work. Ultimately, the other planet either helps or hinders your emotional nature and sense of security.

Conjunctions to Mercury

My desire to communicate unites with the nature of the other planet.

Your thoughts and ideas are affected by the character of the other planet. Everything about your walk and talk is affected. Your ability to think, question, gather information, and communicate is either helped or hindered by the other planet, depending on how you choose to use this connection.

Conjunctions to Venus

My desire to relate and acquire unites with the nature of the other planet.

Your capacity to relate to the world and to others is affected by the temperament of the other planet. Your ability to determine what is of value, as well as your own worth in and out of relationships, is either aided or held up by the other planet. Your connection to the world and everyone in it, as well as physical possessions and financial practicalities, are enhanced or challenged, depending on your awareness and application of this combination.

Conjunctions to Mars

My desire to act and be assertive unites with the nature of the other planet.

Your actions are affected by the nature of the other planet. Your vitality, courage, and ability to act in your own self-interest are all helped or hindered by the other planet. How you process anger and frustration is also affected by your use of this aspect, so you must take every opportunity to use this potent combination in the best way possible.

Conjunctions to Jupiter

My desire to expand into new areas unites with the nature of the other planet.

Your ability to take risks is influenced by the traits of the other planet. Your optimism, philosophy, and ability to explore new ideas and foreign countries are either helped or hindered by the other planet, depending on how you integrate this aspect. Make sure to use this connection in the best way possible as you expand your understanding of yourself and the world.

Conjunctions to Saturn

My desire to achieve and gain respect unites with the nature of the other planet.

Your sense of responsibility and desire to succeed are both affected by the nature of the other planet. Your ability to manifest success on your own terms, achieve a rock-solid sense of satisfaction, and draw on your own wisdom and experience are either supported or undermined by the other planet's agenda. As you work with Saturn conjunctions, you must make mature and sometimes difficult decisions and be patient as you wait for signs of success and validation.

Conjunctions to Uranus

My desire to be unique unites with the nature of the other planet.

Your sense of individuality is affected by the nature of the other planet. Your ability to embrace the new and unusual, as well as to think and act along new lines, is strengthened or weakened by the other planet, depending on your own awareness of this aspect. Since Uranus introduces a rebellious energy to any planetary combination, you must be wary of creating constant but unproductive commotion in this area of your life.

Conjunctions to Neptune

My desire to seek spiritual awareness unites with the nature of the other planet.

Your comprehension of the sacred and the spiritual is affected by the nature of the other planet. Your ability to seek the ideal and follow your own inner vision is enhanced or undermined in very subtle ways by the other planet. You must honor and integrate your intuition with the nature of the other planet.

Conjunctions to Pluto

My desire to be strong and capable of transformative change unites with the nature of the other planet.

Your perception of personal power is affected by the nature of the other planet. Your ability to act as an alchemist in your own life is either strengthened or weakened by the other planet, depending on how you integrate this aspect. Since Pluto conjunctions compel you to combine your craving to transcend your circumstances with another equally powerful part of your personality and experience, you must be particularly aware of the energies at work.

Oppositions: Karmic Confrontations

The bond formed between two planets positioned on opposite sides of the chart is called an opposition. Unlike the emphasis of a conjunction, an opposition compels you to integrate and include two very different parts of your nature and create a greater awareness.

This cosmic conversation forces you to create balance between the two planets in op-position. When two planets confront one another, each creates a separate and opposite pull on different parts of your life. You become aware of the differences between yourself and others. Oppositions suggest issues from past lives that must be resolved in a way that includes an equal amount of each impulse, rather than choosing one over the other.

Oppositions can be downright tricky, because others will quite often step in and play devil's advocate. If we look at Joan of Arc's chart (in the introduction), she has Mercury and Neptune in opposition. Mercury is her desire to communicate, whereas Neptune is her drive to experience heaven on earth. The opposition suggests that she must use both her mind and her spirituality to get her point across, and in many ways she succeeded. However, King Charles VII abandoned her to be tried for heresy in the English courts, even though she had sacrificed a great deal for his cause. In this case, he was reflecting the likelihood of betrayal and disillusionment that occurs when Neptune and Mercury find themselves on opposite sides of the chart.

As you read through your own opposing aspects, consider that planets can be other folks in your life as well as these positive or not-so-positive traits:

Planet	People	Traits
Moon	Mother, family, woman	Emotional sensitivity, moodiness
Sun	Father, man	Pride, generosity, egotism
Mercury	Sibling, coworker, aunts and uncles	Curiosity, analytical, duplicity
Venus	Female lover, wife	Charm, grace, possessiveness
Mars	Male lover, husband	Energetic, motivational, anger, impatience
Jupiter	Doctor, professor, minister, grandchild	Optimistic, expansive, over-whelming energy
Saturn	Boss, authority figure, judge	Maturity, wisdom, fearfulness
Uranus	Friend, associate, political figure	Independence, individuality, rebelliousness
Neptune	Nurse, nun, psychologist	Vision, spirituality, deception
Pluto	Banker, magician, surgeon, criminal	Empowerment, manipulation

Chances are pretty high that this list will help you identify and understand some of the forces at work in your own alliances. Just be careful that you don't get caught up in the blame game and point the finger at your own oppositions as the source of your discontent. Ultimately, the responsibility lies with you to acknowledge and heal the challenging issues that show their ugly faces in the mirror of relationships.

Oppositions to the Sun

I must balance my ego and identity with the energy of the other planet.

Your sense of self stands in stark contrast to the nature of the opposing planet. You must strike a balance between your ego and the force that seems to oppose your pride.

Oppositions to the Moon

I must balance my needs and feelings with the energy of the other planet.

Your emotional needs and sensitivities are confronted by the nature of the planet in opposition to the Moon. You must maintain equilibrium between your feelings and the forces that appear to threaten your security.

Oppositions to Mercury

I must balance my thoughts and ideas with the energy of the other planet.

Your thoughts and ideas seem to oppose the nature of the other planet. You must strive to create a balance between your mental abilities and the forces that seem to counter your ability to get your point across.

Oppositions to Venus

I must balance my desire for relationships and possessions with the energy of the other planet.

Your desire to relate to others and to acquire the necessities and luxuries of life is tested by the character of that planet. You must establish a sense of balance between your capacity to connect and the planetary force that seems to undermine your self-worth.

Oppositions to Mars

I must balance my actions with the energy of the other planet.

Your actions seem to contradict the nature of the opposing planet. You must strike a balance between your natural ambition and the force that seems to contest your courage and bravado.

Oppositions to Jupiter

I must integrate the energy of another planet with my optimism.

Your optimism seems to argue with the personality of the opposing planet. Take advantage of the opportunity to incorporate the cautionary warnings of the other planet with your drive to expand and enlarge your view of the world.

Oppositions to Saturn

I must integrate my sense of responsibility with the influence of another planet.

Your sense of responsibility clashes with the character of the opposing planet. Ultimately, you must strike a balance between your obligations and the force that seems to oppose your success.

Oppositions to Uranus

I must balance my individuality with the force of another planet.

Your individuality stands in stark contrast to the makeup of the opposing planet. It is up to you to find a balance between your innovative approach to life and the force that seems to undermine your innovative ideas and independence.

Oppositions to Neptune

I must balance my idealism with the force of another planet.

There is a great disparity between your own sensitivity and compassion and the spirit of the opposing planet. You must strive to integrate a peaceful relationship between your intuition and the forces that challenge your kindness and concern.

Oppositions to Pluto

I must balance my desire to change with the force of another planet.

Your strength of character contrasts with the temperament of the opposing planet. You are pressed to incorporate both your ability to transform as well as the desires of the planets that seems resistant to it.

Part Two Summary

If you're interested in your karmic journey, now is the time to take a look at your traveling companions. This worksheet provides plenty of room for you to record the specifics from your own chart. Make note of your Sun and Moon signs, which illuminate who you are and what you need, in and out of relationships.

If your Sun is in Aries in the fourth house, refer to the sections "Sun in Aries or in the First House" and "Sun in Cancer or in the Fourth House" in chapter 4. The "Sun in Aries" section tells you to embrace your nature and define yourself. The "Sun in the Fourth House" section points to a need to be emotionally sensitive. The one-liner "cosmic clues" for these sections indicate that you use courage and emotional sensitivity to define yourself. Use the same process to complete the entries for your Moon, conjunctions, and oppositions.

1. My Sun.

   My Sun sign: the best way to let my light shine: _____

   _____

   _____

   Cosmic clue: _____

   My Sun's house: the area of life where I must express the real me: _____

   _____

   _____

   Cosmic clue: _____

My own experiences: _____

_____

_____

2. My Moon.

My Moon sign: my deepest needs:_____

_____

_____

Cosmic clue: _____

My Moon's house: the area of life where I must express my needs: _____

_____

_____

Cosmic clue: _____

My own experiences: _____

_____

_____

3. Cosmic encounters: conjunctions and oppositions.

The inner circle of your chart contains aspect lines that connect one planet to another. These lines tell you what kind of conversation is taking place between the two planets involved. Each line contains a glyph to indicate which aspect is formed between the two planets. For this exercise, look for lines that contain an opposition glyph (☍). Planets that are conjunct are so close together that there's not even room to draw a line between them in the center circle. Look for planets that are very close together in your chart. If the planets are within 4 degrees of one another, you can consider them to be conjunct.

Not all planets will be conjunct and/or opposite another planet. Once you note the conjunctions and oppositions contained in your chart, use this worksheet to better understand the cosmic conversations taking place. Here's a list of planetary keywords to help you on your way:

Planet	Glyph	Primary Impulse
Sun	☉	To create
Moon	☽	To respond, nurture
Mercury	☿	To learn, communicate
Venus	♀	To relate, acquire
Mars	♂	To act, fight
Jupiter	♃	To explore, expand
Saturn	♄	To be responsible
Uranus	♅	To break with tradition
Neptune	♆	To seek out the divine
Pluto	♇	To control your fate

- Conjunctions occur when two planets fall right next to each other and emphasize certain parts of your personality and your karmic journey.

    _____ aligns with _____.

    My desire to _____ blends with my desire to _____.

    _____ aligns with _____.

    My desire to _____ blends with my desire to _____.

    _____ aligns with _____.

    My desire to _____ blends with my desire to _____.

- Oppositions: When two planets are on opposite sides of the chart, they confront one another and form a separate pull on your life force. Oppositions create the opportunity to combine these different parts of your personality, rather than choosing one over the other.

    _____ opposes _____.

    My desire to _____ must be balanced with my desire to _____.

    _____ opposes _____.

    My desire to _____ must be balanced with my desire to _____.

    _____ opposes _____.

    My desire to _____ must be balanced with my desire to _____.

Part Three
Ticket to Paradise

You, too, can find heaven on earth. Good things happen, and when they do, you can bet your chart is bursting at the seams thanks to the bounty of three nifty gift-bearers in your chart. The key to making good things better is to count your blessings and make the best use of your spiritual gifts each and every day.

Before you read through the next few chapters, take a moment to check your chart for these points:

- *Jupiter:* The enormous mass of this planet should give you a clue as to the amount of good things it promises in your life.
- *Part of Fortune:* Gee, even the name sounds good.
- *North Node:* the secret passageway that prompts you to follow your bliss.
- *Trines and sextiles:* cosmic combinations between planets that map out your field of dreams.

Jupiter is the ultimate well-seasoned traveler, passing through a multitude of cultures and philosophies with the greatest of ease. His job in your chart is to remind you that there is a world of opportunity out there, if you're willing to leave your comfort zone behind and consciously quest for adventure.

The Part of Fortune (⊗) is one of those astrological terms that actually makes sense. It's the quick ticket to fun and luck, yours for the taking. The North Node (☊) is also full of promise, but since its blessings are even bigger and better, it requires more effort on your part. More on that later.

Trines and sextiles are heaven's way of reminding you that life is sweet, or at least it should be. A trine in your chart identifies a special blessing or talent that you have at your disposal. In Joan of Arc's chart, Mercury, which is her desire to learn and communicate, trines Mars, her desire to act and assert herself. She had a gift for being straightforward in her thoughts and comments, as well as the ability to motivate others with her message. Sextiles work in much the same way, with the exception that you have to make a conscious effort in order to experience the full benefit.

The even better news about all of these blessings and bounty in your chart is that you can consciously strengthen their influence. Embrace the higher vibes of their potential and you can increase their impact in no time at all. Once you get the ball rolling, there's no telling how far you will go.

7
Jupiter

You Can Never Have Too Much
of a Good Thing

Big, wide, wonderful Jupiter acts as a travel guide in your chart, mapping out the wonders of your world. Jupiter just loves to do things in a big way, and his role in your chart is to make sure you are pursuing bigger and better goals as you travel along your life's path.

Whenever you crave more passion and joy in your life, rest assured that Jupiter is speaking to your soul. When you answer the call to live large, Jupiter pays off in a big way. In fact, Jupiter's sign and house highlight the lucky streak in your chart. The more you work it, the luckier you get. What a deal!

On the other hand, Jupiter is by no means subtle, and he loves to egg you on and cajole you into taking a flying leap. The good news is that Jupiter, much like a guardian angel, will help you land on your feet even if you happen to fall.

Jupiter in Aries or in the First House

My opportunities lie in taking action in my own self-interest and in honoring the gift of courage.

With Jupiter in Aries, you have an immense desire to be the best and brightest, no matter what you do. You are the great explorer, out the door in a flash and on to conquer the undiscovered country before anyone else has begun to pack their bags. You've been blessed with an abundance of courage, bravado, and outright audacity to see you on your way. You do best when you give free rein to your impulse to escape the limitations of partnerships and get out there and do your own thing.

On a personal level, others look at you as impatient and impulsive, but they secretly adore and envy your incredible sense of self-confidence. Of course, you love the attention and flattery, but the minute it limits your options and fences you in, Jupiter prompts you to pull the plug and move on. Seek out companions who complement, rather than compete with, your nature.

The big picture with Jupiter in Aries is that your soul is set to lead, not follow. That may sound pretty nifty from the outset, but you will succeed only if you honor your innate bravado and cultivate your belief in yourself.

Jupiter in Taurus or in the Second House

My opportunities lie in being self-reliant and in developing my values.

With Jupiter in Taurus, you have an intense connection to the physical realm. All of your adventures are grounded in the desire to master and manipulate the material world. You've been endowed with an innate understanding of the laws of nature, but Jupiter's quest is to expand your understanding of your own nature, independent of all that stuff your surround yourself with. You do best when you choose to establish and incorporate a strong sense of values into your life and accomplishments. Jupiter in Taurus promises great opportunities when it comes to prosperity, but without values, you will simply end up buried beneath the profusion of possessions that you have so diligently acquired.

In personal relationships, you are as good as gold. Unfortunately, you attract more than your fair share of those who would gladly relieve you of your bounty and blessings. In these situations, you must compare your own worth as opposed to your apparent assets. That's exactly the side trip that Jupiter hoped you would take, so that you could build your philosophy on your own self-worth rather than the fickle fluctuations of a portfolio filled with stocks and bonds.

Ultimately, Jupiter is paving the way for you to experience all the physical joys that life has to offer. Others may envy the ease and effortlessness with which you grow and multiply your assets, but it all adds up to nothing unless you embrace the sacred truth that you already have everything you need.

Jupiter in Gemini or in the Third House

My opportunities lie in questioning my world and keeping my options open.

With Jupiter in Gemini, your mind is brimming with questions, and you look at life as an endless adventure, flitting from one exciting idea to another. You've been blessed with loads of curiosity and mental agility to see you on your way. You do best when you allow your consciousness to zig and zag in your quest for information and understanding. You may not get all the answers, but Jupiter promises a pretty exciting ride along the way.

Your inquisitiveness is both charming and irritating to others. Partners mistakenly hope that you will eventually light upon a topic that will hold your interest for more than a heartbeat. With Jupiter in Gemini, it is your questioning nature, not the answers, that enriches the lives of your pals and partners. When others attempt to clip your wings, follow your instincts and fly off on your next adventure.

Jupiter in Gemini is like having an unlimited number of frequent-flyer miles that can be cashed in at any time. You can go anywhere, anytime. Of course, all that freedom sounds lovely, but only if you honor the sacred contract that you're here to experience the ever changing kaleidoscope of the world with every step you take.

Jupiter in Cancer or in the Fourth House

My opportunities lie in nurturing and nourishing myself and honoring my emotions.

With Jupiter in Cancer, your journey begins in the heart of your emotions, where you must sort out the instincts and inklings that subtly guide you along your way. As you prepared for this journey, Jupiter gave you a double scoop of sensitivity and sympathy. Consequently, you occasionally find yourself adrift in a sea of needs, not knowing where to start as you flounder in a world of others' wants and wishes. Jupiter in Cancer suggests that you start closer to home and that you'll do much better once you start taking care of yourself and your own desires.

In intimate relationships, it's easy for the other person to think of you as an all-accepting, all-loving parent instead of a partner who has needs of his or her own. Fortunately, Jupiter can get you back on track if you look closely at prospective partners and look for that all-important ability to take care of him- or herself. If there's no self-reliance to be found, your best bet is to reclaim your space and tend to your own needs.

Jupiter's grand plan is for you to achieve the ultimate emotional high. That may sound better than warm cake from the oven, but you won't get anywhere near that summit unless you consciously listen and act as your soul reveals your own wants and wishes.

Jupiter in Leo or in the Fifth House

My opportunities lie in being true to myself and in developing my creativity.

With Jupiter in Leo, you are driven to take center stage in your personal and professional lives. You've been blessed with plenty of charisma and a hearty helping of leadership ability to see you on your way. You prosper when you pursue your passions, not in a self-centered or egotistical way, but in a way that warms and inspires others to achieve some level of greatness.

On a personal level, others look at you as a never-ending font of self-assurance and poise. Jupiter has booked passage for you through some pretty wild and woolly adventures, and you can walk the gauntlet with nary a scratch. Unfortunately, others dismiss your own doubts and misgivings just when you and your creativity could use a boost. In that disappointing moment, Jupiter drives his point home: when you are caught up in a storm of uncertainty, you must reach deep into your heart and fuel your future with the sacred fire within.

Ultimately, Jupiter is paving the way for you to get the appreciation and adoration you are seeking. However, that applause will be so much white noise if you don't respect yourself and the life you have created.

Jupiter in Virgo or in the Sixth House

My opportunities lie in putting my world in order and honoring my desire to make a difference.

Jupiter in Virgo reveals that you signed up for the work-study plan in order to fund your journeys this time around. You have a great capacity to manage a multitude of different projects and activities, and you've been blessed with plenty of practicality to see you on your way. You do best when you can see that your efforts make a substantial difference. However, with this many balls in the air, you must learn to look past the inevitable errors and use Jupiter's generous outlook to forgive yourself for your very human imperfections.

On a personal level, others look at you as ready and willing to do whatever it takes to get the job done. Unfortunately, this placement can find you stuck with most of the work as others dilly and dally their way along. Avoid the temptation to pick up people who are projects. Don't waste your time with those who can't pay the light bill on time or who never quite stopped living with mom. You'll do best when you look for others who are as dedicated to excellence in the key areas of life as you are.

In the end, Jupiter paves the way for you to experience divine right order. How exactly will that happen? All you have to do is to recognize the heavenly perfection of your life, right here, right now.

Jupiter in Libra or in the Seventh House

My opportunities lie in keeping my own life in balance and in choosing what is best for me.

With Jupiter in Libra, you have been blessed with enough charm and grace to soothe the savage beasts that cross your path. You're in love with love, and nothing makes you happier than to see a romance unfolding, especially in your own life. Offers for adoration abound, but Libra constantly reminds you that life is not supposed to be a conveyer belt of relationships. No, with Jupiter in well-balanced Libra, you do best when you make sure that there's plenty of time and space for yourself, as well as others, in your life.

Others observe the apparent ease and grace with which you navigate the world and figure you have enough good manners to go around and that they can leave their own good graces at home. Consequently, you are quite often mismatched with someone whose values and ideals are sadly out of sync with your own. When in doubt, look for partners who put on their best face for you and follow it up with kindness and consideration.

At the end of the day, Jupiter provides the opportunity for you to have the perfect relationship with a great guy or gal. That idea may seem fantastic as well as unreachable until you realize that Jupiter is inspiring you to venture into that most foreign of territories—a loving relationship with yourself.

Jupiter in Scorpio or in the Eighth House

My opportunities lie in honoring my strength and power.

With Jupiter in Scorpio, your soul chose this lifetime to master yourself and your power—not exactly a modest aspiration. This placement bestows strength, tenacity, gut instincts, and the incredible ability to read people and their problems. Of course, it's up to you whether you use these gifts for good or evil, but this placement is especially karmic, so remember, what goes around, comes around. Consequently, you'll benefit most when you surround yourself with those who will willingly support and empower you, rather than those who need to be manipulated to move off of ground zero.

In intimate exchanges, others see you as having ultimate control, able to turn lead into gold and transcend the most difficult of situations. This leads to situations where you make things better for anyone and everyone else and end up with nothing left when it comes to addressing your own trauma and troubles. As you wander the labyrinth of relationships, look for someone who is seeking to strengthen his or her own skills rather than drain you dry.

Jupiter is inviting you to escape the mind games and power plays that plague your everyday life. He's reminding you that in terms of your own power, you can either use it or lose it, and that you can only use it if you reach deep down into your consciousness and make peace with your shadow.

Jupiter in Sagittarius or in the Ninth House

My opportunities lie in exploring my world and expanding my consciousness.

Jupiter in Sagittarius blatantly suggests that you had one thing on your mind when you chose this lifetime: adventure. You have every intention of thinking big and living even larger. To see you on your way, Jupiter has filled your backpack with all sorts of goodies, such as a really big desire to explore, a huge need to go on a quest, plenty of passion to pursue whatever you fix your mind on, and lots more. Forget the folks who piously proclaim that bigger isn't necessarily better; you know that you can never have too much of a good thing. However, life isn't one holiday after another, so you'll do better with this placement when you search for the sublime, even when you are stuck in traffic.

Since Jupiter is at home in Sagittarius, it's easy to attract attention with this fantastic combo. Because it's such a stupendous mix, others see you as unstoppable and unbeatable. In fact, you are sure to run headlong into closed doors and missed opportunities. As you're strolling down Relationship Road, look for someone who is already on his or her own adventure. That way, your partner will have plenty of sympathy when you run into problems.

Every step of the way, Jupiter wants to see you having the time of your life. What's the catch? Only that you need to open up to the options that abound in your everyday life, rather than looking out at the horizon and putting your happiness on hold for another day.

Jupiter in Capricorn or in the Tenth House

My opportunities lie in accepting greater responsibility and in honoring my own wisdom.

With Jupiter in Capricorn, you are obliged to construct a life in which you become a success on your own terms. Capricorn provides you with plenty of care and concern, caution and conscientiousness, but it's up to you to utilize these gifts. You have the enviable ability to make things happen and manifest on the physical plane. Jupiter's lesson in this lifetime is that the ultimate achievement is to become your own authority. Oh sure, you could give in to the Capricorn's tears and fears, as Jupiter blows them way out of proportion. But it's really up to you to overcome the obstacles and attain your distant dreams by consistently moving toward them.

Some folks look at you and wonder if there's no end to the amount of work you can fit into a day. As a result, your relationships are littered with people who figure that since you're doing such a great job, why should they help? You'll need to search for souls who are mature and responsible in their own right, and are not looking for someone to take care of them.

Ultimately, Jupiter just wants you to know when to say when, so you can enjoy your season of sweet success. How exactly do you do that? By honoring that wise and wily part of your soul that reminds you that success on anyone else's terms isn't success at all.

Jupiter in Aquarius or in the Eleventh House

My opportunities lie in exploring and embracing the unusual and unknown.

With Jupiter in Aquarius, you have a penchant for intellectual freedom, and you've been blessed with a super-sized helping of intelligence and logic to see you on your way. You do best when you break free of the rigid beliefs that have shaped your family for generations and go on to explore new concepts. In this position, Jupiter blesses you with all the tools to be a teacher, if you're willing to take a risk and put yourself and your knowledge out there.

On a personal level, others look at you as a guru and listen intently as you expound on your latest philosophy. Unfortunately, partners, parents, friends, and lovers grow frustrated as you unexpectedly jump the tracks and head off in a quirky new direction. They will talk to you about settling down and putting down roots, but you and your Jupiter will have none of it. When in doubt, extract yourself from associations that become stifling or overwhelming.

Ultimately, Jupiter is paving the way for you to share your insights with others. This sounds like a sweet job, but only if you honor this blessing by continually replenishing your intellect and experience with the new and the unusual.

Jupiter in Pisces or in the Twelfth House

My opportunities lie in increasing my spiritual understanding and in developing my intuitive gifts.

With Jupiter in Pisces, your tender dream of heaven on earth includes putting an end to war, famine, hunger, broken nails, and dirty dishes. There's no doubt about it—you're an ethereal person living in a material world, and you're not about to give up your closely guarded visions of Utopia. Jupiter's extravagance in the land of fantasy fuels your hunger to combine with the divine and to hitch a ride on the celestial express. To see you on your way, Jupiter in Pisces, just like every good fairy godmother, has granted you three wishes: all the intuition, vision, and compassion you could possibly want. While those really are lovely gifts, you can sure get sidetracked with all that sensitivity.

Others envy the mystique that graces your life, and before you know it, your life is littered with folks who are searching for a lucky break. Jupiter in Pisces reminds you that you just need to release these ne'er-do-wells and utter a silent prayer of your own as you actively seek out someone who has plenty of faith to believe in his or her own good fortunes.

Of course, Jupiter has booked passage for you on the ship of dreams. But to make sure you're in the right place at the right time, you must listen to the whisperings of your own intuition to ensure that you don't miss the boat.

8
Part of Fortune
Good and Plenty

If an astrologer were to take your Sun, Moon, and Ascendant and render them down to one simple message, the Part of Fortune would be it. It's the quickest and easiest way to pinpoint the nature of the blessings and miracles that light your path.

What's the catch? Only that you make the most of your potential in your everyday life. In other words, when in doubt, return to the message contained in your Part of Fortune, and life will get better and better.

Part of Fortune in Aries or in the First House

My straightforward actions enhance my life.

An Aries Part of Fortune blesses you with the ability to take charge and boldly move into new and unfamiliar areas of life. Make no apologies for the true-blue warrior within who is seeking truth, justice, and a new challenge around every corner. With this placement, it is important for you to take action and move forward in ways that boost your self-confidence.

You can get downright frustrated if the folks around you become complacent and shy away from confrontation. However, it's important to listen to their concerns about peace, and remember that this is the principle that is propelling you onward.

Part of Fortune in Taurus or in the Second House

My consistent disposition enhances my life.

The Part of Fortune blesses you with an unparalleled capacity to stick with it and see things through to the blissful or bitter end. You have an innate strength and the ability to create enduring stability wherever you go. To make the most of the Part of Fortune in Taurus, make sure to stand your ground and embrace the consistent rhythm that shapes your life.

You may be surrounded by those who desire change simply for the sake of change and openly disapprove of the status quo that you preserve. Even so, their ideas and attitudes remind you of the necessity to allow yourself to change things along the way, especially when they add value to your projects.

Part of Fortune in Gemini or in the Third House

My curiosity enhances my life.

Why is the sky blue? This is a simple childhood question, but for you, these kinds of questions are important. The Part of Fortune blesses you with an innocent curiosity about the world and those around you. With this placement, it is important for you to actively wonder and wander through life, as though seeing it for the first time.

However, you may find that you are surrounded by those who are either disinterested in questioning themselves and their world or who arrogantly assert that they already know enough. While these may seem like foreign concepts, there is some value to knowing when to quell your restless inquisitiveness and understanding when you have arrived.

Part of Fortune in Cancer or in the Fourth House

My emotional sensitivity enhances my life.

The Part of Fortune blesses you with an open kindness that invites others to seek out your gentle sensitivity. You are able to nurture and nourish, and it is important for you to be emotionally engaged with others, not only for their benefit, but to be on the receiving end as well.

With the Part of Fortune riding the tides of Cancer, others around you may speak of the importance of maturity and wisdom. That's not to say that you aren't wise or mature. However, you must draw on your own emotional understanding to empower others to be personally responsible for their own lives rather than dependent upon the kindness of others.

Part of Fortune in Leo or in the Fifth House

My generosity enhances my life.

The Part of Fortune in Leo blesses you with a big heart and an even bigger spirit eager to include others in life's passionate adventure. You love and lust with great abandon, and live for the moment. In order to sustain your life force, you must be excited by what you are doing and the life you are creating.

Occasionally, you are surrounded by those who speak of perspective and beg you to stop and think before you lunge into your next escapade. This is not a bad idea, since it offers you a chance to step out of the immediacy of the moment, look at the big picture, and realize just how fun and exciting your life really is.

Part of Fortune in Virgo or in the Sixth House

My gentle dedication enhances my life.

The Part of Fortune in Virgo blesses you with the understanding that beneath the apparent chaos of life, there is a plan and purpose for your existence. Your abilities to organize and analyze, examine and evaluate, allow you to comprehend the sacred subtleties of life. Virgo reminds you that the divine is deeply hidden within the duties and activities of everyday life.

You may be surrounded by those who urge you to go with the flow and drift along. Of course, this aimless wafting and wandering doesn't really appeal. However, relinquishing the diatribe of details that litter your path can truly simplify your life.

Part of Fortune in Libra or in the Seventh House

My sociable nature enhances my life.

The Part of Fortune in Libra blesses you with the ability to gracefully connect and collaborate with others. Your natural charm and apparent ease around others offers you plenty of opportunities for loving liaisons and professional partnerships. Libra reminds you that no man is an island and that the quality of your relationships shapes your existence.

As you navigate the web of relationships, others preach the seemingly selfish philosophy of taking care of yourself first and foremost. While this may seem terribly arrogant, there is great value in the concept of actually being yourself rather than adapting and acquiescing your authenticity out of existence.

Part of Fortune in Scorpio or in the Eighth House

My intensity enhances my life.

With the Part of Fortune in Scorpio, you have a natural talent to get to the heart of the matter and to slash through the emotional issues that could easily clog and clutter your consciousness. You are direct and forthright, and it is this clarity that enables you to move through life with an innate sense of preordained providence. Scorpio's emphasis puts you on a first-name basis with the inevitable passages of life and death.

The Part of Fortune in Scorpio adds no small measure of transition and transformation to your world. In the eye of this storm, others will prompt you to choose a well-measured life of predictable patterns. While that is not your path, you can certainly hold up this serene scene as an ideal to reach for as you are mapping the extremes of human experience.

Part of Fortune in Sagittarius or in the Ninth House

My quest for knowledge enhances my life.

The Part of Fortune in Sagittarius blesses you with a no-holds-barred enthusiasm to explore the world. You seek and search for the unfamiliar and undiscovered territory and passionately pursue a greater understanding of yourself as well as the human race. Sagittarius propels you onward and upward, and reminds you that your soul longs for adventure.

Occasionally, you encounter those who cling to the comforts of home and think you should too. They smugly suggest that everything you need is right around the corner and go on to remind you that a rolling stone gathers no moss. You must honor your innate desire to constantly expand your boundaries. Embrace the fact that it is the journey, rather than the destination, that satisfies your soul.

Part of Fortune in Capricorn or in the Tenth House

My ambition enhances my life.

The Part of Fortune in Capricorn is incredibly helpful when it comes to accomplishing great things and increasing your bottom line. Your ability to manage and manifest quickly moves you into positions of greater responsibility. However, Capricorn forces you to acknowledge your obligations as well as your karmic duties along the way.

When you pursue success on your own terms, others suggest that your real responsibilities lie closer to home. Of course, you are capable of tender feelings and gentle emotions, but you can quickly drown in their dangerous undertow. Ultimately, you must honor your aspirations and carefully integrate the emotional desires that lie buried in your own heart and soul.

Part of Fortune in Aquarius or in the Eleventh House

My intellect enhances my life.

The Part of Fortune in Aquarius arms you with enough intelligence and perspective to understand the big picture of your own life. You even have flashes of insight about the future of humankind.

As you pursue unusual and oddball thoughts while keeping others at arms' length, there's no end to others' observations that you are cool and reserved. Their well-meaning ideas suggest that you should really get more involved and live in the moment, rather than being zoned out contemplating the future. Maybe that's not such a crazy idea, since you must live in the present to change the future.

Part of Fortune in Pisces or in the Twelfth House

My intuition enhances my life.

The Part of Fortune in Pisces infuses your existence with a direct line to a higher authority. You are able to hook in to spiritual consciousness and wander through the mundane world all the while maintaining a sense of the mystical and magical.

You may be surrounded by those who prompt you to get real, and to get a real job, for that matter. They poke and prod with their comments about practicality and common sense, but at the end of the day, your faith never falters. However, if you consistently apply some of the plans and programs that they promote, there's no doubt that you can boost your intuitive gifts.

9
North Node
Secret Passageway to Success

The symbol for the North Node (☊) looks like an ornate doorway. Like any doorway, you have to make the conscious decision to walk through it and discover what is on the other side. The North Node points to the mindful shifts that you must make in order to be truly happy. The North Node's message rarely feels comfortable, as it compels you to get out of your rut. The good news is that once you move out of your comfort zone, you will discover a new dimension of joy and opportunity—not a bad tradeoff.

North Node in Aries or in the First House

I am happiest when I assert myself.

The North Node in Aries prompts and prods you to assert your true personality into every interaction you encounter. This isn't about being selfish and self-centered. Instead, you must learn the fine art of being true to yourself without overpowering your partner.

This is quite a challenge, since Aries is not your comfort zone. In this case, you must overcome your complacency and tendency to acquiesce. Instead, you are challenged to create a stronger sense of self. The house where the North Node is located will tell you in which area you must assert yourself. Ultimately, though, you need to conquer your fears and affirm your inner courage in every aspect of your life.

North Node in Taurus or in the Second House

I am happiest when I am self-sufficient and develop my own values.

The North Node in Taurus induces and encourages you to make your own way in life. You need to support yourself and prioritize your wants and needs. On the other hand, this does not suggest that you should turn into a suspicious old scrooge, selfishly hoarding whatever comes your way. In essence, you must decide what is and what isn't of value to you, so that abundance can bless your life and the lives of others.

Taurus is not exactly your comfort zone, and it's much easier to fall back on the support of others. The house where the North Node is located will tell you in which area you are called upon to develop your values and establish self-reliance. When in doubt, look inside yourself for resources and solutions, and affirm your own strength and stability.

North Node in Gemini or in the Third House

I am happiest when I explore my options.

The North Node in Gemini tempts and teases you to learn more about yourself and your own little corner of the world. Gemini asks you to walk your talk and talk your walk. In other words, words are what it's all about, but it's up to you to make sense of it all.

The fluttery nature of Gemini is far from your comfort zone. Instead, you prefer to live in the world of the rhetorical and theoretical, focusing on one principle or philosophy at a time. The house where the North Node is located will tell you in which area you must discover and explore the world with an open and questioning mind. To make the most of the North Node in Gemini, you should enjoy the wonder of the world around you. Accept that your curiosity and inquisitiveness grant you full admission to the amusement park of life.

North Node in Cancer or in the Fourth House

I am happiest when I nurture myself and am sensitive to others' needs.

The North Node in Cancer nags at you to acknowledge and act on your feelings. You must dive headfirst into the world of emotions and recognize the necessity to tend to all of your needs—physical, mental, emotional, and spiritual.

The tender sensitivities of Cancer are not your comfort zone. You would much rather return to the professional world of respect and recognition, but the North Node in Cancer now demands that you direct that professional wisdom toward managing the softer side of your soul. The house where the North Node is located will tell you in which area you must be sensitive, both to yourself and to others. To embody the North Node in Cancer, embrace the gentle ebb and flow of emotions, and affirm that your sensitivity and sympathy are the signposts that guide you on your path.

North Node in Leo or in the Fifth House

I am happiest when I play and develop my creative abilities.

The North Node in Leo invites you to come out and play. You must bound into life with unbridled passion, so that your creativity can blossom. On the other hand, you are not the only actor on life's stage, so you must learn to encourage others' lights to shine as brightly as your own.

After lifetimes of standing apart from life's passions, the easy confidence of Leo is simply not your comfort zone. The North Node in Leo beckons you to join the dance, to exit your ego, and to open your heart to passion's promise. The house where the North Node is located will tell you in which area you must actively ensure that you are having fun. When in doubt, stop the busyness of your life, have a moment of fun, and affirm that joy and happiness are your divine right.

North Node in Virgo or in the Sixth House

I am happiest when I establish order and rhythm in my life.

The North Node in Virgo insists that you get organized and take care of your own concerns, rather than sacrificing your soul and yourself to enable others. Let your own well-ordered life be a faultless model, and resist the temptation to criticize others if they falter or fail.

Virgo's obsession with order and organization as the path to perfection is definitely not your comfort zone. It's much easier to hope and pray for the best, instead of taking the necessary action to keep your life on track. The house where the North Node is located will tell you in which area you must establish a sense of order. At the end of the day, you must surrender to Virgo's clear and concise agenda for your life, and affirm that order simply clears the way for peace and harmony to grace your life.

North Node in Libra or in the Seventh House

I am happiest when I seek harmony in my partnerships.

The North Node in Libra bids you to find the perfect balance between you and your partner, you and the world. This is not exactly an easy task, but if you honor this instinctive need for contact and collaboration, you will find contentment both in and out of relationships.

Even so, Libra and its constant pining for pleasant partnerships is not your comfort zone. It's so much easier to stomp off in a huff and do your own thing, instead of navigating the complex world of companionship. The house where the North Node is located will tell you in which area you must consciously seek out the invaluable input from others. You will reap the greatest benefits when you actively choose to link up with others and embrace the blessings that relationships bring into your life.

North Node in Scorpio or in the Eighth House

I am happiest when I actively seek meaningful experiences.

The North Node in Scorpio makes a powerful statement in your life and empowers you to seek out sacred understanding of life and its mysteries. The problem is that the depth of spiritual secrets is so mesmerizing that others often mistake your intensity for an unhealthy desire to control and manipulate.

Controlling the transformational energy of Scorpio is not one of your favorite things. In fact, it's much easier to stick with the tried and true and let sleeping dogs lie. However, the cosmos consistently contrives to compel you to explore your own strength as well as the support you can gain from others. The house where the North Node is located will tell you in which area you must draw upon your inner strength and accept the support of others. To make the most of the North Node in Scorpio, embrace your talent to transform and transcend your world.

North Node in Sagittarius or in the Ninth House

I am happiest when I move away from the familiar and expand my understanding of the world.

The North Node in Sagittarius encourages and invites you to journey into new, uncharted territory in the many different areas of your existence—mental, physical, spiritual, and emotional. You must be ready to roam at the drop of a hat, but that doesn't give you a free pass to be capricious and uncaring.

The wild wanderlust of Sagittarius is definitely not your comfort zone, and it's easy to scatter your energy on random projects and silly sidelines. Instead, you must focus on a single course of action. The house where the North Node is located will tell you in which area you must literally search far and wide. To get the full benefit from the North Node in Sagittarius, make sure to appreciate the part of your soul that longs for adventure and happily harbors great expectations.

North Node in Capricorn or in the Tenth House

I am happiest when I take myself and my objectives seriously.

The North Node prompts and prods you to get out and make something of yourself. But it has to be on your terms. Of course, Capricorn mandates that you be prudent in planning your path and that it's a wise idea to seek advice from others who have already achieved a high standard of success.

Capricorn's serious, ambitious nature is not your comfort zone, and you must overcome your natural sentimentality and sensitivity to create a strong foundation for your hopes and dreams. The house where the North Node is located will tell you in which area you must develop more maturity and become successful in your own right. Ultimately, though, you need to listen to your own wisdom and actively pursue your own achievements, regardless of others' expectations.

North Node in Aquarius or in the Eleventh House

I am happiest when I embrace and express my own unique viewpoints.

The North Node in Aquarius advises you to think outside the box and actively embrace progress. This unconventional approach can quickly lead you to act in an erratic and volatile way. You will need to monitor how your actions affect others and their opinions of you.

In many ways, the cool intellect of Aquarius is not your comfort zone, and it's easy to fall into old patterns of forcing your personal views on others rather than maintaining your perspective. The house where the North Node is located will tell you in which area you must consciously acknowledge your individuality and independence. The North

Node in Aquarius will be most effective when you embrace the simple fact that you must break with tradition and move independently into your future.

North Node in Pisces or in the Twelfth House

I am happiest when I seek out spiritual experiences.

The North Node in Pisces draws you into a search for spirituality, and you can quickly dilute your soul's purpose if you allow yourself to coast along and claim you are no longer responsible for the details of your life.

The gentle, flowing nature of Pisces is not your comfort zone, and you would much rather return to the well-ordered world of past lives. However, in this lifetime you have chosen to search out the subtle whisperings of god and the cosmos rather than rely on the clockwork efficiency of man and his methods. The house where the North Node is located will tell you in which area you must use your intuition and have faith that there is more to life than what you can see. As you work with your North Node in Pisces, it is essential to take the time to listen to the hum and buzz of heaven above.

10
Trines and Sextiles
Advantageous Associations

Trines and sextiles are the fast track to bountiful blessings. They're so darn nifty that many astrologers sign their e-mails wishing the recipient "trines," which is astrologese for "good luck."

Trines and sextiles offer you an uncluttered expressway to getting what you want. With a trine, the energy flows between the two planets in a gracious and graceful waltz. The sextile is a scaled-down version of the trine and offers an opportunity, if you're willing to work long and hard to achieve great things. Remember that each planet represents a specific kind of drive or desire in your soul. Trines and sextiles are often associated with talents and blessings, so you can use the chart below to quickly identify your own treasure trove of good things from on high.

Planet	Type of Talent/Blessing
Sun	Creativity, self-confidence, children
Moon	Emotional, familial
Mercury	Mental agility, physical activity

Planet	Type of Talent/Blessing (continued)
Venus	Charm, attractiveness
Mars	Action, drive, initiative
Jupiter	Optimism, philosophical
Saturn	Maturity, wisdom
Uranus	Independence, individuality
Neptune	Visual capacity, intuitive
Pluto	Personal power, strength

These points help you understand your own path to success that much better. Either way, this is the prime time to check your chart and figure out how you can step it up a notch to enjoy the blessings and bounty of heaven.

Trines and Sextiles: Spiritual Blessings and Opportunities

Trines and Sextiles to the Sun

The way I express my creativity is enhanced by the other planet.

In past lives, you used your creativity in a positive way. Now, as you express your identity, you are given free passage by the connecting planet and experience a certain ease and grace. Trines and sextiles to your Sun offer creative talents and self-confidence, and it is up to you to consciously integrate their blessings into your everyday life.

Trines and Sextiles to the Moon

The way I express my feelings is enhanced by the other planet.

In past lives, you used your emotional energy in a constructive way. Now, as you express your emotions and needs, you enjoy a certain ease and grace as you incorporate the energy of the other planet. Trines and sextiles to your Moon provide increased emotional confidence and security, especially as you honor your sensitivity and sentimentality as gifts and talents in your everyday life.

Trines and Sextiles to Mercury

The way I express my thoughts is enhanced by the other planet.

In past lives, you learned to question your world and think for yourself. This time around, you find it especially easy to give voice to your thoughts, especially when you combine the character of the other planet. Trines and sextiles to your Mercury offer endless options for you to wander and wonder about the world around you. And, of course, the more you use these positive connections, the better your life gets every day.

Trines and Sextiles to Venus

The way I express my values is enhanced by the other planet.

In past lives, you used your charm and grace in ways that not only improved your own life but brought peace and harmony to the lives of others. In this lifetime, your relationships and finances are eased according to the influence of the other planet. You will find even more contentment as you actively incorporate their blessings into your everyday life.

Trines and Sextiles to Mars

The way I express my drive is enhanced by the other planet.

Your actions and deeds in past lives exhibited the epitome of courage and bravado. In this life, you find that your ability to take action is given free passage by the energy of the other planet. In past lives, you used your creativity in a positive way. Now, as you proceed along your path, you can find an even greater vitality and sense of self as you vigorously mix your own energy with the talents of the other planet.

Trines and Sextiles to Jupiter

The way I express my philosophy is enhanced by the other planet.

In past lives, you developed your higher mind and cultivated an optimistic outlook. Now, the connecting planet provides an easy way for you to express your philosophies and to enjoy a certain level of protection as you take risks. Of course, trines and sextiles to Jupiter just get bigger and better when you embrace their bounty into your everyday consciousness.

Trines and Sextiles to Saturn

The way I express my sense of responsibility is enhanced by the other planet.

Despite challenges, obstacles, and hardships in past lives, you fulfilled your obligations and even made it look easy. Does that buy you time off for good behavior in this lifetime? Not exactly. However, it definitely gives you an edge when it comes to working smarter, not harder, especially when you judiciously combine the energy of the connecting planet as you complete the tasks along your path, big and small.

Trines and Sextiles to Uranus

The way I express my individuality is enhanced by the other planet.

In past lives, you were the harbinger of change, which wasn't always easy, since you may have ended up on the wrong end of a firing squad. Your commitment to truth over political correctness has earned you certain rights in this lifetime, such as expressing yourself and your views of the future. Now, whenever you stand out from the crowd and live to tell about it, you can thank the planets that trine or sextile your Uranus.

Trines and Sextiles to Neptune

The way I express my idealism is enhanced by the other planet.

In past lives, you used your compassion in a truly enlightened way. Now, as you express your search for heaven on earth, the planets that sextile and trine your Neptune part the Red Sea for you. The mystical and magical are that much closer, thanks to these positive connections in your chart. Neptune is the god of smoke and mirrors, so make sure that you're not fooling around and fooling yourself as you incorporate these trines and sextiles into your life.

Trines and Sextiles to Pluto

The way I express my desire to change is enhanced by the other planet.

You used your personal power, as well as your ability to empower others, in a potent way in past lives. This time around, you have a constant conduit of strength surging through your endeavors, especially as you incorporate the essence of the planets that trine and sextile your Pluto.

Part Three Summary

1. Jupiter.

   Whenever you crave more passion and joy in your life, rest assured that Jupiter is speaking to your soul. When you answer the call to live large, Jupiter pays off in a big way. In fact, Jupiter's sign and house highlight the lucky streak in your chart.

   Jupiter's sign: the nature of my opportunities and talents: _____

   _____

   _____

   Cosmic clue: _____

   Jupiter's house: the area of my life enhanced by Jupiter: _____

   _____

   _____

   Cosmic clue: _____

   My own experiences: _____

   _____

   _____

2. Part of Fortune.

   Use the sign and house of your Part of Fortune to pinpoint the nature of the blessings and miracles that will light your path.

Part of Fortune sign: how I can attract blessings
and good fortune in my life: _____

_____

_____

Cosmic clue: _____

Part of Fortune house: where I can attract blessings
and good fortune in my life: _____

_____

_____

Cosmic clue: _____

My own experiences: _____

_____

_____

3. The North Node.
   The North Node's message compels you to get out of your rut and indicates the conscious shifts that you must make in order to be happy.

   North Node sign: the type of action
   I need to take to find happiness: _____

   _____

   _____

   Cosmic clue: _____

   North Node house: where I need to
   make conscious shifts: _____

   _____

   _____

   Cosmic clue: _____

My own experiences: _____

_____

_____

4. Trines and sextiles.

The inner circle of your chart contains aspect lines that connect one planet to another. These lines tell you what kind of conversation is taking place between the two planets involved. For this exercise, look for lines that have either a trine (△) or sextile (✶). Not all planets will have trines and/or sextiles. Once you note the sextiles and trines contained in your chart, use this worksheet to better understand the cosmic conversations taking place. Here's a list of planetary keywords to help you on your way:

Planet	Glyph	Primary Impulse
Sun	☉	To create
Moon	☽	To respond, nurture
Mercury	☿	To learn, communicate
Venus	♀	To relate, acquire
Mars	♂	To act, fight
Jupiter	♃	To explore, expand
Saturn	♄	To be responsible
Uranus	♅	To break with tradition
Neptune	♆	To seek out the divine
Pluto	♇	To control your fate

Trines and sextiles offer you an uncluttered expressway to getting what you want. With a trine, the energy flows between the two planets in a gracious and graceful waltz. The sextile is a scaled-down version of the trine and offers an opportunity, but you have to put a bit of work into it.

_____ trines _____.

My desire to _____ enhances my desire to _____.

_____ trines _____.

My desire to _____ enhances my desire to _____.

_____ trines _____.

My desire to _____ enhances my desire to _____.

_____ sextiles _____.

My desire to _____ builds on my ability to _____.

_____ sextiles _____.

My desire to _____ builds on my ability to _____.

_____ sextiles _____.

My desire to _____ builds on my ability to _____.

Part Four
Getting Derailed

The heavens wouldn't be doing us a favor if everything in our charts promised that life would be fairy-tale perfect. In fact, if you're old enough to be reading this book, chances are you've already experienced your fair share of delays and disappointments. While the gods and cosmos are not necessarily intent on hurling obstacles your way, astrology can help you comprehend the complications that you will likely encounter on your journey. Your chart can even point out the consequences of not owning up to your fears and tears. The heavens provide plenty of strategies to simplify your spiritual progress and avoid unnecessary pain and heartache.

Before you read through the next few chapters, take a moment to find the following points in your own chart:

- *Saturn:* Think of his rings as celestial barbed wire, fencing you in till you learn your lessons.

- *Part of Karma:* Just like it sounds. What goes around, comes around.

- *South Node:* a treasure trove of talents and past-life abilities to access at any time.

- *Squares and quincunxes:* cosmic combinations between planets that point out, in no uncertain terms, the changes and challenges you must address in this lifetime.

Astrologically speaking, Saturn makes no bones about the fact that you have a job to do and a karmic responsibility to do it well. If you're willing to do the work, Saturn rewards you with unshakable self-confidence as well as the respect and admiration of others—not a bad tradeoff for putting your nose to the grindstone and your shoulder to the wheel.

Understanding your Part of Karma will serve you well if you're willing to face up to its implications. While its theme is often sobering, it also holds the keys to the karmic kingdom. To reap the benefits, you must respect the fact that everyone, even you, has a cosmic closet crammed full of unfinished business.

The South Node is chock full of good things from lives gone by. That's the good news. On the other hand, it's full of everything gone by, even the unsavory stuff. The best way to describe the challenge of the South Node is to think about Uncle Fred telling the same story over and over again. The first time you heard it, it was great, but by the tenth time, you were sick to death of it. That's the South Node at work, and you can get just as old and irritating as Uncle Fred if you don't watch your step.

Squares and quincunxes are not exactly the most popular aspects at a cosmic cocktail party, because they chafe and challenge you to change your path. Depending on the rest of your chart, you may or may not take to that idea right off the bat. Planetary dialogue that results in squares and quincunxes isn't always the easiest information to digest. On the other hand, squares and quincunxes ignite your imagination and spark your consciousness with more than enough initiative to change your life.

These parts of your chart clarify your lessons and karmic challenges. You may even get some confirmation as to why certain parts of your life are so difficult to master. But don't stop there. The real payoff comes when you step up to bat and take a good, solid swing at fulfilling your karmic contracts. Who knows? You may even hit a home run.

11
Saturn
Grow Up and Move Up

If ever there was a planet in need of a good spin doctor, Saturn is it. Plagued by centuries of bad press, Saturn is rarely seen in a good light, mainly because he has no patience for immaturity. His message is simple: If you want to stop splashing around in the kiddy pool, you need to take off your water wings, show up for swimming lessons, and eventually dive into the deep end. In other words, if you want to achieve in any area of your life—whether it's a diet or a doctorate—you need to utilize Saturn's slow-but-steady formula for success.

Saturn's placement in your chart points to the part of your experience where you are most likely to experience delays and a sense that the cosmos is holding out on you. It's also an area in which you must face your fears and overcome any sense of inadequacy. Fortunately, Saturn's placement promises big payoffs if you're willing to work hard and long at achieving great things.

Saturn in Aries or in the First House

I succeed when I am assertive and courageous.

Saturn in Aries indicates that your past lives deprived you of a sense of self and that your ability to assert yourself and your ideals was severely restricted. Over and over again, your identity was eclipsed by your friends and lovers. As a result, one of your karmic lessons is to define and refine your sense of self. You must use the innate wisdom and discipline of Saturn to do what is right for you, regardless of how unpopular those choices make you. Saturn's nature mandates that progress in this area may be slow but will reward you with an unshakable self-image.

Saturn's requirement for prudence and caution rains on your parade whenever you become impatient or selfish. On the other side of the coin, Saturn will just as quickly trip you up if you spend too much time and energy making life better for everyone else in your life. Instead, Saturn suggests that you apply common sense and recognize that your primary responsibility is to yourself.

Saturn's house placement identifies the area of your life where you must be mature and responsible, and apply your ambition in terms of being yourself. As you gain experience and master this lesson, you will be favored with success and recognition in this area, and you will realize a lasting spiritual fulfillment.

Saturn in Taurus or in the Second House

I succeed when I rely on myself and my values.

Saturn in Taurus suggests that your ability to earn your own money and own your own stuff was seriously restricted in past lives. Your money and resources were constantly controlled and manipulated by others who weren't exactly kind and nurturing. Consequently, one of your karmic lessons is to make your own way and make up your own mind. Despite the difficulties you face, you must use the innate wisdom and discipline of Saturn to establish your own financial foundation and ascertain the value of thoughts and things. Saturn's no-nonsense approach mandates that progress in this area may be slow but will reward you with an enduring sense of self-worth, independent of your bank balance.

Saturn's requirement for prudence and caution rains on your parade whenever you become possessive or overly protective of your stuff. Conversely, Saturn will trip you up if you rely too heavily on financial support or emotional sympathy from others. Saturn simply wants you to use some common sense and recognize that your principal responsibility is to create stability in your own life.

Saturn's house placement identifies the area of your life where you must be wise when it comes to financial interactions with others, as well as where you must overcome a sense of inadequacy or poor self-worth. As you gain experience and master this lesson, you will experience great success and recognition in this area, and you will realize a lasting sense of security.

Saturn in Gemini or in the Third House

I succeed when I see my ideas through to fulfillment.

Saturn in Gemini indicates that your past lives may not have provided you with many options to learn and that your experiences were somehow restricted to a very small arena. Consequently, one of your karmic lessons is to continue to feed and expand your mind. You must use the innate wisdom and discipline of Saturn to balance your thoughts and actions and recognize that while progress in these areas may be slow, it will pay off in the end.

Saturn's requirement for prudence and caution can rain on your parade when negative or fearful thoughts undermine your bright ideas. You must guard your beliefs and opinions and realize that wrong thinking can undermine your success. On the other hand, being flippant and sarcastic won't accomplish anything either.

As you get older, you will find that your well-thought-out ideas are taken seriously and lead to a greater sense of success and spiritual fulfillment. Saturn's house placement identifies the area of life where you must ask questions, think things through, and apply your common sense in order to succeed.

Saturn in Cancer or in the Fourth House

I succeed when I am sensitive to my own and others' needs.

Saturn in Cancer implies that your past lives lacked the emotional comforts of hearth and home. A life without love is bleak indeed, and even the gods above wouldn't blame you if you shut down emotionally. Your ability to figure out what others needed, let alone interpret your own feelings, was severely restricted. Your sensitivity was repeatedly obscured by immense responsibilities and obligations. Now, one of your karmic lessons is to tend to domestic needs, namely yours. Apply Saturn's inherent wisdom and discipline to consistently meet your emotional needs, even if others see that as selfish. While Saturn's temperament suggests that progress in this area may be slow, it also promises to reward you with a lasting sense of emotional security.

Saturn throws a wrench in your plans whenever your emotional insecurities take center stage or you deny your own needs and vulnerabilities. Saturn will just as quickly trip you up if you invest too much of your emotional resources meeting the needs of others. Instead, Saturn suggests that you use common sense and recognize that your chief responsibility is to acknowledge and act upon your own needs.

Saturn's house placement identifies the area of your life where you must be emotionally mature and responsible. You will be favored with success and a rock-solid sense of security in this part of your life as you integrate the emotional lessons of Saturn in Cancer.

Saturn in Leo or in the Fifth House

I succeed when I lead with my heart.

Saturn in Leo indicates that your past lives provided precious little joy and delight in your everyday existence. Your capacity to direct your own destiny and create your own life was severely restricted. Over and over again, your heartfelt desires were eclipsed by duties to an overbearing person who lorded his or her position of authority over you. Therefore, one of your karmic lessons is to learn to simply have fun and to take pleasure in your own soul. This is easier read than done, because your heart simply isn't in it. In this enigmatic arrangement, Saturn requires you to apply wisdom and discipline to the process of pleasure and to regularly schedule fun and frivolity. This practice is sure to garner some sideways glances from others in your life, but nevertheless, Saturn's prerequisites are clear: play and passion are the primary pathways to success.

Of course, you must be cautious about living only for the moment and becoming a slave to the latest craze. On the other side of the coin, Saturn will just as quickly trip you up if you spend too much time and energy trying to make sure that others pursue their passions, instead of enjoying your own life in progress. Instead, you must apply common sense and recognize that your primary task is to honor your own soul and be a bright, shining example to others.

Saturn's house placement identifies the area of your life where you must accept responsibility and take the lead. As you gain experience and master this lesson, you will be favored with success and recognition in this area, and you will realize a lasting spiritual fulfillment.

Saturn in Virgo or in the Sixth House

I succeed when I use my analytical ability to decide what is best for me.

Saturn in this position indicates that in past lives your everyday activities were controlled by others and your ability to determine the pattern of your life was severely restricted. Over and over again, your natural desire to live your life according to your own schedule was eclipsed by a commitment to some larger purpose or cause. As a result, one of your karmic lessons is to honor your inner agenda and to create a personal plan for success. Saturn's innate discipline reminds you that you must deal with the realities of everyday life, including paying the light bill and stocking the pantry. In your search for stability through organization, your obsession with order and analysis can overwhelm even the most practical of friends. However, Saturn's nature promises that while you may not perfect your life immediately, you will indeed find grace in the process of everyday activities.

Saturn's disciplinary nature becomes crystal clear the minute you reach out to impose your particular methods onto others. And Saturn will just as quickly call you to task if you spend too much time and energy cleaning up others' messes. Instead, Saturn advises that you must be practical and use your resources to honor and order your own world.

Saturn's house placement identifies the part of your life where you must be mature and responsible, and acknowledge your objective to live according to your own rules. As you master this lesson, you will find success, recognition, and spiritual satisfaction.

Saturn in Libra or in the Seventh House

I succeed when I form lasting partnerships with those who honor me.

Saturn in this position indicates that you lacked the opportunity to create healthy relationships in your past lives and that it is a challenge to connect with those who honor and respect you. Over and over again, your sense of equilibrium was eroded by the unfair actions of others. Consequently, your karmic lessons involve the delicate interaction between you and another person. Of course it would be easy to charm and acquiesce, but Saturn compels you to search for relationships where you can be your real self, all the while demanding true partnership. Sure, this might make you downright unpopular, as you enforce a higher standard on yourself as well as your partner, but Saturn does grant eventual success in relationships, especially when you look for a mate rather than a master.

If you take Saturn in Libra to the extreme and keep track of every exchange using a tit-for-tat mentality, Saturn will be quick to point out the need for grace and harmony. On the other hand, Saturn will just as quickly trip you up if you spend too much time and energy crusading for others' rights and sticking your nose into another person's business. Instead, Saturn mandates that you apply common sense and recognize that your primary responsibility is to develop well-balanced connections with others.

Saturn's house placement identifies the area of your life where you must be mature and responsible, and seek out trustworthy partners. As you master Saturn in Libra, you will reap great benefits, both personally and through your relationships.

Saturn in Scorpio or in the Eighth House

I succeed when I use my strength to create powerful shifts in my life.

Saturn in Scorpio indicates that your ability to change yourself and your life was seriously challenged in your past lives by an overemphasis on preserving and protecting your material wealth and security. Now, your capacity to draw upon your power to transform and transcend the concrete structures of your workaday world feels constrained. One of your karmic lessons is to embrace change and its inherent chaos as a path to spiritual power and success. Saturn requires you to delve into the psychological needs that motivate your deepest hunger. Skipping this step will quickly result in slogging through the fallout of change, simply for the sake of change. However, if you conscientiously apply Saturn's prudence and caution to the evolution of your soul, you will establish a rock-solid sense of personal power.

The minute you start using Saturn in Scorpio to manage and manipulate the karma or destiny of others, Saturn is quick to put you back on the straight and narrow. Saturn will just as easily trip you up if you spend too much time and energy pointing out others' karmic lessons. Instead, Saturn mandates that you employ common sense as you familiarize yourself with your own soul's power.

The house placement of Saturn in Scorpio determines the area of your life where your soul must make itself over and move up to a higher vibration. As you gain expertise and master this lesson, you will be blessed with success, recognition, and lasting spiritual power in this part of your existence.

Saturn in Sagittarius or in the Ninth House

I succeed when I explore new, uncharted territory.

Saturn in Sagittarius suggests that in past lives you lacked freedom of thought and action and that your ability to explore new concepts in philosophy and religion was severely restricted. Over and over again, your desire to venture into uncharted territory was hampered by a narrow-minded estimation of your potential. Either you sold yourself short, or others simply didn't want to recognize your potential. Now, one of your karmic lessons is to learn to think for yourself. You must apply Saturn's inherent discipline to break free of petty ideas and belief systems and consciously consider the thoughts and beliefs that shape your view of yourself and your world, even when these choices draw bigoted criticism from others.

Once you develop a new view of the world, you must curb Sagittarius' tendency to puff yourself up with all-knowing pride, all the while expecting others to worship you as some kind of guru. On the other hand, Saturn will frown upon you the minute you start seeking out gurus in a misguided belief that they somehow know what's right for you. Saturn forces you to return to the simple truth that you must acknowledge and act upon your own beliefs, rather than blindly following the pied piper.

Saturn's house placement identifies the area of your life where you must integrate new ideas and concepts in order to achieve lasting success. As you gain knowledge and master this lesson, you will establish an unshakeable sense of personal freedom, backed by a continuing quest for knowledge and understanding.

Saturn in Capricorn or in the Tenth House

I succeed when I recognize my own authority and wisdom.

Saturn in Capricorn indicates that your past lives were shaped by great responsibilities and obligations and that your ability to succeed on your own terms was severely limited or controlled by others. Your authority, even in personal affairs, was challenged by rules, regulations, difficulties, and dilemmas. After lifetimes of delay and disappointment, you must use Saturn's discipline to overcome the obstacles that stand in your way in your personal and professional affairs. Others may misunderstand your motives when you focus on your own success and overcome your trials and tribulations. However, Saturn promises that you can achieve a rock-solid sense of satisfaction that is sure to fill your soul.

The minute you use Saturn's drill-sergeant discipline to supervise others on their own karmic paths, Saturn will quickly admonish you to stick to your own task. More importantly, you must draw upon an inner wisdom to recognize that not everything is your responsibility, even though you are more than capable of finishing the job. Conversely, Saturn will not be amused if you choose to look to others to direct your destiny. Nope, you and you alone are accountable to travel the peaks and valleys of your own karmic path.

Saturn's house placement names the part of your life where you must continuously be ready for inspection. However, as you become more confident in your own sense of wisdom, Saturn will reward you with success, acknowledgment, and an enduring certainty of your soul's true purpose.

Saturn in Aquarius or in the Eleventh House

I succeed when I am independent of the influence of others.

Saturn in Aquarius indicates that your free speech and independent action were limited in past lives and that your view of the future was constantly challenged by others who clung to old, outmoded institutions. In this life, your soul has decided to think outside of the box and break with tradition, but that doesn't necessarily make you the most popular person around. Now, your restless mind has boundless opportunities to shock and surprise others with your new-fangled ideas, if you're willing to stand out in a crowd. Don't think that gives you license to become a crank. Instead, you must be cautious and careful as you introduce new ideas and concepts, whether you're looking to change your career or change the world.

Saturn suggests that you tame the rattled restlessness of Aquarius and admonishes you whenever you advance change merely for the sake of change. On the other hand, Saturn will just as quickly trip you up if you spend too much time and energy hanging out as a nameless face in a crowd of wannabes. Instead, Saturn in Aquarius reminds you that your primary responsibility is to enjoy the freedoms of this lifetime and make good use of them.

Saturn's house placement points to the spot in your life where you must introduce new ideas and break old, outmoded patterns. As you become more proficient in handling Saturn in Aquarius, you will discover great satisfaction in knowing that you have the capacity to change your own mind as well as the opinions of those around you.

Saturn in Pisces or in the Twelfth House

I succeed when I listen to my intuition.

Saturn in Pisces indicates that in past lives you lacked the opportunity to pursue spiritual experience and understanding throughout your life and that your sensitivity and intuition were restricted. Over and over again, your compassion and sympathy were eclipsed by some greater call to sacrifice yourself. Now, you must employ the innate wisdom and discipline of Saturn to listen and make sense of your impressions and instincts, even though others may look on with disdain and impatience. Of course, your first response to this statement is that your intuition doesn't work for you. That's precisely it. You must move past lifetimes of conditioning in which you used your compassion for everyone else's benefit and begin to use it to your own advantage.

Saturn has installed a fail-safe mechanism of sorts in this placement. It's easy for you to be overwhelmed by the needs and agendas of others, and you quickly search for some peace and quiet. If you sit still for long enough in the silence and solitude, the subtle promptings of Saturn in Pisces will surface in your own consciousness.

Saturn's house placement identifies the part of your existence where you must consciously seek the still, small voice of wisdom. But Saturn is never happy with just listening. Once you know what you need, you must take constructive action in this part of your life. Then you will find spiritual fulfillment as well as secular satisfaction as you move forward on your own path.

12
Part of Karma
No Pain, No Gain

The role of the Part of Karma in your chart is to give you a heads-up about what you intend to resolve when it comes to the unfinished business from past lives. Its message is derived from the combination of your Ascendant, Saturn, and Sun. Remember that your Ascendant represents your starting line for this lifetime. Imagine being ready to sprint and having a ton of bricks fall down around you. That would be Saturn. And to make sure you get the point loud and clear, your ego and personality both have to take a back seat. In other words, the Part of Karma is the no-frills discussion of your spiritual responsibilities this time around. It even outlines specific challenges that force conscious consideration and a mature, responsible approach.

The Part of Karma isn't a walk in the park, but the more you incorporate its message into your awareness and actions, the more you will benefit from providence at critical turning points in your life. The Part of Karma is closely linked to Saturn, so you'll do well to heed Saturn's directives in your own chart.

Part of Karma in Aries or in the First House

I must learn to project my true self and take responsibility for my actions.

Your past lives were littered with failures and foibles as your soul swung between the extremes of absolute self-annihilation and hostile aggression. Now, your soul is in search of your long-lost sense of self and the ability to act in your own self-interest without starting a world war. Armed with nothing more than your own courage and bravado, you face the ultimate battle of honoring and expressing the true you.

Karmic circumstances and situations compel you to develop a more mature outlook on yourself and your life. When you step up to the plate, intent on fulfilling the responsibilities indicated by your Part of Karma, you will reap the blessing of a strong sense of self that stands the test of time.

Part of Karma in Taurus or in the Second House

I must learn to earn my own way and take responsibility for my values.

In past lives, you may have neglected your material responsibilities, ignored your financial obligations, or focused on your financial status to the point that everything and everyone else suffered in your life. As a result, in this lifetime you must perfect your ability to be self-sufficient and to be a good steward of your material goods.

Fateful shifts prompt you to establish financial security and values, be responsible, and live up to your commitments. As you move through life, you begin to understand the role that financial security and resources play in your physical as well as your spiritual life. However, it is as you move consciously to fulfill the responsibilities indicated by your Part of Karma that you reap the blessings of self-worth and the ability to be self-sufficient.

Part of Karma in Gemini or in the Third House

I must learn to communicate and take responsibility for my thoughts.

Your past lives are characterized by your thought patterns, good and bad. In some situations, you may have focused solely on getting information, but failed to use it. In other lives, your mind was dead set against any new-fangled ideas and innovations. Now the Part of Karma reflects your soul's desire to comprehend the power of your mind to shape or shatter your existence.

You frequently encounter spiritual circumstances and situations that constantly challenge your capacity to learn and communicate. When you fulfill the obligations implied by your Part of Karma, you'll quickly see the benefits. For when you open your consciousness, gather new information, think things through, and explore the wonders of the world, your soul is refreshed, your mind is renewed, and your body is ready for fun and games.

Part of Karma in Cancer or in the Fourth House

I must learn to identify my feelings and take responsibility for my needs.

Emotional expression in your past lives was severely restricted and controlled, either by your own fears or by your circumstances. Now, the Part of Karma in Cancer presents specific lessons that induce emotional growth and expression. You must rely on your feelings and instincts in order to navigate the uneven emotional waters that you encounter throughout your life.

Your life path includes spiritual circumstances and situations that challenge your forward progress and help you develop emotional wisdom. As you move through this lifetime, you will be continually dared to acknowledge, embrace, and integrate your needs as you confront emotional and domestic challenges. However, it is only as you honor the ebb and flow of emotions in your life that you will find the security your soul hungers for.

Part of Karma in Leo or in the Fifth House

I must learn to find joy in life and take responsibility for what I create.

Past lives were devoid of excitement and creativity, either due to your own detachment or situations that prevented the pursuit of pleasure. Or perhaps your past lives were filled with one party after another to the point that you lost the ability to anticipate or even get excited. Now your soul is seeking to regain that lost joy, passion, and lust for life and to take your own passions seriously.

Spiritual circumstances and situations that advance your creative capabilities and compel you to search out your heart's desire will surface as you move through your life. However, it is as you move consciously to discharge the responsibilities indicated by your Part of Karma that you reap the blessings. As you open your soul to the delights of this life, your capacity for fun will brighten your own existence and bring blessings into the lives of those around you.

Part of Karma in Virgo or in the Sixth House

I must learn to make meaningful contributions and take responsibility for the details in my life.

In past lives, you shied away from dealing with the practical responsibilities of daily life for a variety of reasons, including the search for spiritual perfection, a sense of inadequacy, or restrictions in your health. In this lifetime, your soul is intent on dealing with the mundane details as well as devoting your efforts to a worthwhile cause.

A multitude of mystical situations will test your ability to make a substantial difference in your own life on earth and tempt you to drop out of the rat race. However, the Part of Karma confirms your soul's notion that this is the perfect time to deal with the here and now. Through constantly focusing on the details of your existence, you will be blessed with a sense of divine right order that brings heaven to earth.

Part of Karma in Libra or in the Seventh House

I must learn to form well-balanced relationships and take responsibility for my choices.

Your past lives were filled with unresolved, inequitable relationships plagued by control issues and a lack of true partnership. Now, your soul is looking for real relationships, but first you have to recognize that you are an important part of the equation in the give and take of collaboration.

Several challenging and confusing situations will make you confront the lack of balance that undermines any area of relationships, including physical, emotional, spiritual, or financial. While it is tempting to believe that you are "destined" to have such relationships, progress will happen only when you consciously deal with the challenge to make inequity a thing of the past. Then you will be blessed with the sense that you can indeed develop divine partnerships as you move through your karmic journey.

Part of Karma in Scorpio or in the Eighth House

I must learn to draw on my inner strength and take responsibility for change in my life.

Past lifetimes were filled with power struggles that boiled down to a single creed: control or be controlled. This left your spirit spent and karmically indebted to others. Now your soul longs to transcend this ongoing fight for life.

Difficulties and delays challenge you in this lifetime to transform your use of power and resist the temptation to use others and manipulate situations in your favor. By consciously identifying the areas of life where you must use your own power in an appropriate way, or where you may encounter difficult power struggles with others, you will overcome the past and take pleasure in blessings that come your way. Finally, as you take control of your own shadow, you will make tremendous strides in your own soul's evolution.

Part of Karma in Sagittarius or in the Ninth House

I must learn to move beyond my comfort zone and assume responsibility for the risks I take.

In past lives, you may have traveled very narrow and well-worn paths, both physically and philosophically, that ultimately took you nowhere. Now, your soul is on a quest to expand your understanding and shake off the shackles of tradition.

Fated circumstances frequently compel you to consider the issues of personal freedom and the need to explore your world. While it would be easy to blame your situation, you must take the high road, and conscientiously study and develop an expanded understanding of your world and your own role within it. As you do, you will be blessed with the opportunity to venture into unknown territory in your life and enjoy the heady experience of risking it all.

Part of Karma in Capricorn or in the Tenth House

I must learn to manage important projects and take responsibility for my fears and shortcomings.

The rubble of unanswered obligations and long-forgotten duties in past lives makes this Part of Karma particularly burdensome, as it creates a seemingly endless list of work to be done. Your soul chose this lifetime to endure the restrictions and restraints and develop self-discipline in order to reap the benefits of fulfilling its responsibilities.

Karmic situations and spiritual circumstances poke and prod you to make things happen. You must consciously put your shoulder to the wheel and do everything possible to ensure that a job is well done. However, as you focus on manifesting success, you will be rewarded with a strong sense of self-confidence and the confirmation of being on the right path.

Part of Karma in Aquarius or in the Eleventh House

I must learn to adopt objective viewpoints and take responsibility for my idiosyncrasies.

In past lives, you shied away from standing out in a crowd or showing off your genius. Now, your soul is on a mission to express as much independence, individuality, intelligence, and innovation as it possibly can this time around.

Predestined challenges repeatedly remind you to embrace your differences rather than attempt to fit in. On the other hand, you must resist the temptation to create unrest or rebel against the system just for the sake of stirring things up. Instead, you must consciously apply Aquarius's logic as you institute change, whether on a personal level or in your professional life. The payoff is that you'll make tremendous progress as you break old soul patterns and open your higher mind to new, exciting experiences.

Part of Karma in Pisces or in the Twelfth House

I must learn to use my intuition and take responsibility for my spiritual understanding.

In past lives, you may not have paid much attention to the ideas and inklings that flooded your consciousness, and this oversight cost you dearly. Now, your soul is bound and determined to integrate the mystical into the mundane aspects of life and longs to have faith, not only in a higher power but also in your own intuition and visions.

Over and over again, the cosmos contrives to put you in the center of circumstances in which you must honor your hunches. You must consciously integrate your instincts with your intelligence and seek to live a life that reflects your inner vision. However, as you learn to use your sixth sense, you will be in the right place at the right time as your own great expectations get that much closer to becoming a reality.

13
South Node
Secret Well of Strength and Fortitude

The symbol for the South Node (☋) looks like an ornate urn. Think of it as the keeper of your past-life strengths and triumphs. That's the good news. The bad news is that it's so much easier to loll about in the glory days of the past than to move forward with the business of vanquishing new venues. When you consider the strengths outlined by the South Node, think of them as a reserve to be drawn on, but if you constantly tap into this supply, it will soon be drained dry. To understand how to balance the South Node, review the insights offered by your North Node, in chapter 9.

South Node in Aries or in the First House

I am most comfortable when I am acting on my own, but it's also easy for me to act selfishly.

With the South Node in Aries, you are naturally outgoing, direct, and capable of rushing in where angels fear to tread. There's no doubt that your raw courage serves you well over the course of your life. However, you need to be cautious of being too impatient with the world and everyone in it. Focus instead on encouraging yourself and others to act assertively rather than aggressively.

The house placement of your South Node indicates the part of your life affected by your brothers in arms and kindred spirits from past lives. Your North Node in Libra points the way to making the most of your well-developed ability to bravely face new challenges.

South Node in Taurus or in the Second House

I am most comfortable when my life is stable and structured, but it's also easy for me to resist change.

With the South Node in Taurus, you have a great capacity to be sure and steady, to the point that your life becomes incredibly predictable. You easily establish habit and routine and pragmatically keep an eye on the bottom line. While the capacity to create constancy serves you well over the course of your life, you must be aware that sticking with the tried and true will lead you to a dull and boring life. However, you can empower yourself and others to create a rock-solid sense of self-worth so that life's inevitable changes do not undermine self-confidence.

The house placement of your South Node identifies which part of your life will be populated by soul mates and kindred spirits from past lives. Your North Node in Scorpio guides you in making the most of your well-developed ability to develop resources, both for yourself and for others.

South Node in Gemini or in the Third House

I am most comfortable when my life is full of variety and choices, but it's also easy for me to scatter my energies.

With the South Node in Gemini, you are a natural communicator, curious about the world and everyone in it. You easily gather bits and pieces of information from the most unlikely of sources. You can shift gears and change pace effortlessly in any area of your life, personal or professional. Of course, all of this comes in handy, but you need to be cautious of being flighty and unfocused. In many ways, you must use your natural curiosity to lead you away from the familiar and out into the big, wide, wonderful world.

The house placement of your South Node indicates the part of your life where you are likely to meet up with soul mates and kindred spirits from past lives. Your North Node in Sagittarius helps you overcome your tendency to spread yourself too thin and still maintain your childlike wonder of the world.

South Node in Cancer or in the Fourth House

I am most comfortable when I am nurturing others, but it's also easy for me to be emotionally temperamental.

With the South Node in this position, you effortlessly navigate through emotional waters with compassion and sensitivity. These traits serve you well over the course of your life. However, you need to be cautious of being too reliant on your own family situation or creating situations in which you become the "little mother" to whom everyone runs in times of stress. Focus instead on empowering yourself and others to act with emotional wisdom rather than neediness.

The house placement of your South Node indicates the part of your life where you are likely to encounter soul mates and kindred spirits from past lives. Your North Node in Capricorn provides the instructions on how to preserve your emotional instincts while achieving great things.

South Node in Leo or in the Fifth House

I am most comfortable when I take pride in myself, but it's also easy for me to be self-centered.

With the South Node in Leo, you have a strong presence and easily command the attention of those around you. You take great pride in yourself and your creations and are easily offended by others' lackluster responses. Your natural ability to lead and inspire others thrusts you into the limelight, but you must be wary of putting too much emphasis on your individual position and losing your awareness of your role in the big picture of life. You must learn to be gracious and allow others to have their moment in the sun.

The house placement of your South Node in Leo indicates the part of your life where you are likely to encounter soul mates and kindred spirits from past lives. Your North Node in Aquarius offers a gift in its cool rationale and altruistic understanding of the divine potential that is only attained through working together for the good of everyone.

South Node in Virgo or in the Sixth House

I am most comfortable when I focus on the practical aspects of life, but it's also easy for me to be overly critical.

With the South Node in Virgo, you are most at ease creating order out of chaos. After lifetimes of analyzing and prioritizing, you have a gift for finding the method in the madness of life, and you find great joy in being able to point to the work you've done.

However, this can quickly lead to a lifetime focused on the mundane rather than the meaningful experiences of your existence. Consequently, you must draw the line when your ability to scrutinize is no longer adding value to your life or the lives of those around you.

The house placement of your South Node indicates the part of your life where you are likely to encounter soul mates and kindred spirits from past lives. Your North Node in Pisces reminds you that in order for you to find the perfection that your soul seeks, you must balance your practicality with the tender sensitivity of kindness and compassion.

South Node in Libra or in the Seventh House

I am most comfortable when I am in partnership with another person, but it's also easy for me to lose my identity.

With the South Node in Libra, you can charm the socks off of just about anyone, which means you can end up involved with lots of folks who aren't quite to your liking. You repeatedly find yourself in one seemingly karmic relationship after another, but that doesn't guarantee happiness and bliss. On the contrary, until you focus on being true to yourself, you will rarely find a partner who is in sync with your soul.

The house placement of your South Node in Libra indicates the part of your life where you are likely to encounter soul mates and kindred spirits from past lives. Your North Node in Aries signals that you must assert yourself and take care of number one, and the relationships will take care of themselves.

South Node in Scorpio or in the Eighth House

I am most comfortable when I empower others to change, but it's also easy for me to manipulate others.

With the South Node in Scorpio, you can move among the bastions of power and control with great cunning and skill. Your ability to read others, as well as their motives, is second nature, and it's easy for you to mastermind any number of plots and plans as long as they preserve your sense of control. Of course, this can all be on the up and up, but you still need to resist the temptation to manipulate the lives and times of others.

The house placement of your South Node identifies the part of your life where you will likely come upon soul mates and kindred spirits from past lives. Your North Node in Taurus forever reminds you of the folly of assuming that your power comes through anyone or anything outside of your own self-worth.

South Node in Sagittarius or in the Ninth House

I am most comfortable when I am free to venture outside of my home territory, but it's also easy for me to be a know-it-all.

With the South Node in Sagittarius, you have an innate sense of being well traveled and well-read and take great pleasure in taking on the role of the guru. You love it when others consult you about any number of subjects, but you can easily fall into the trap of needing to appear that you know it all and then being unable to ask questions. Instead, you need to draw on your ability to inspire and incite others to search for their own truths, rather than relying on the opinions of others.

The house placement of your South Node indicates the part of your life where you are likely to encounter soul mates and kindred spirits from past lives. Your North Node in Gemini entices you to honor your curiosity, and see what new and wonderful adventures it takes you on.

South Node in Capricorn or in the Tenth House

I am most comfortable when I am in a responsible position, but it's also easy for me to be harsh and reserved.

With the South Node in Capricorn, you can easily assume command and find great contentment whenever you are in a position to master and manage your own fate. You value a job well done, and while you expect great things from others, you expect no less from yourself. However, this combination can find you stressing the importance of structure and discipline and overriding your gut feelings.

The house placement of your South Node indicates the part of your life where you are likely to encounter soul mates and kindred spirits from past lives. Your North Node in Cancer helps you understand that accomplishment without contentment is nothing more than going through the motions. Then, when you consult your feelings and respect your needs as you move through life, you will indeed accomplish great things.

South Node in Aquarius or in the Eleventh House

I am most comfortable when I am involved in group projects that utilize my intelligence and perspective, but it's also easy for me to be distant and detached.

The South Node in Aquarius suggests that you have spent lifetimes honing your intelligence and working toward the greater good. After all of this interaction, you are approachable and affable, up to a point. It's easy to keep folks at arm's length, but you can easily appear erratic or prickly in even the closest of connections. Instead, you must use Aquarius's perspective to maintain your outlook and encourage others to do the same.

The house placement of your South Node identifies the part of your life where you are likely to encounter soul mates and kindred spirits from past lives. Your North Node in Leo invites you to engage your mind and excite your passions as you explore more intimate settings and personal relationships.

South Node in Pisces or in the Twelfth House

I am most comfortable when I am compassionate toward others, but it is also easy for me to sacrifice and lose my sense of self.

With the South Node in Pisces, compassion and sympathy flow through your very being. You are intuitive, sensitive, and capable of great understanding and empathy. These qualities are so deeply ingrained that you can't imagine yourself being any other way. However, you need to be cautious of being a pushover and being easily taken advantage of by those who would use and abuse you. Focus instead on empowering yourself and others to act with kindness and grace, but be willing to recognize and refuse the unacceptable behavior that tests your resolve.

The house placement of your South Node in Pisces indicates the part of your life where you are likely to encounter soul mates and kindred spirits from past lives. Your North Node in Virgo can help you stay on the straight and narrow by establishing the ritual of order and organization in your everyday life.

14
Squares and Quincunxes
Roadblocks and Detours

Sometimes you and your best-laid plans hit the wall. As you pick yourself up and dust yourself off, it's only natural to ask yourself what happened. Of course, your chart has plenty to say on the matter as well. The roadblocks and detours reflected by the squares and quincunxes in your chart provide the lowdown on the inevitable obstacles that everyone runs up against.

Squares and quincunxes can make you feel as though the gods and cosmos have a chip on their shoulder when it comes to granting you what you wish for. In reality, squares and quincunxes are just as much a part of success as anything else in the chart. They just have the unsavory job of pointing out that you need to watch your p's and q's along the way.

The upside to squares and quincunxes is that the harder you work at mastering the conflict and challenges that they bring to your door, the better life gets for you. If you look at the charts of successful folks, you'll notice right off the bat that their charts are not made up of blissful, beautiful influences. It is because they emerge victorious over these internal conflicts in their charts that they are able to achieve great things in their public life.

To make the most of your squares and quincunxes, remember that each planet represents a particular spiritual urge to push forward and overcome difficulties and disappointments. Squares and quincunxes relate to rites of passage and supply the conduit through which you can rise to higher levels in all areas of your life.

Planet	Desires, Urges, and Experiences That Are Frustrated, Challenged, Tested
Sun	Creativity, self-confidence, children
Moon	Emotional, familial
Mercury	Mental agility, physical activity
Venus	Attractiveness, relationships, earnings, physical possessions
Mars	Action, drive, initiative, libido, anger
Jupiter	Personal freedom, optimism, philosophy, religion, travel
Saturn	Maturity, wisdom, career, interaction with authority figures
Uranus	Independence, individuality, group interactions
Neptune	Intuition, spiritual understanding, compassion, psychological makeup
Pluto	Personal power, strength, support from others

As you identify the planets that square or quincunx each other in your chart, consider the challenges that these interactions create in your chart. Remember, too, that the real challenge is not the actual difficulties described by these conflicting connections, but remembering that they are simply challenges rather than predestined portents of failure.

Squares: Fateful Challenges

When planets square each other, they reflect two parts of your soul that are at odds with each other. The presence of squares indicates that you intend to resolve this conflict in this lifetime. However, just like riding a bike or learning to ask someone out on a date, chances are you're not going to get it right on the first try. That's why squares have such a reputation for being difficult. In actuality, squares are just like a fire hose full of water pressure. You can either learn to control the power that flows through it, or you can lose your grip on it and get whipped around by situations and circumstances that seem unfair and unjust.

Squares to the Sun

My creativity and self-expression are challenged and tested by the nature of the other planet.

Your ego and your ability to lead are at odds with the agenda of the planet that squares your Sun. You are constantly challenged to take charge of the friction and frustration that pit your spirit against another part of your makeup. Squares to your Sun can strengthen your creative drive and personal charisma when you own up to your inner conflicts.

Squares to the Moon

My emotional nature is challenged and tested by the nature of the other planet.

Your ability to nurture yourself and others is in conflict with the character of the other planet. You must take responsibility for meeting your needs, despite the apparent obstacles reflected by the other planet. As you acknowledge your inner doubts as well as the challenges that block your path, squares to your Moon can actually fortify your emotional defenses and help you create a deeper sense of security.

Squares to Mercury

My mindset is challenged and tested by the nature of the other planet.

Your ability to concentrate and converse is blocked or challenged by the nature of the other planet. You must overcome the tension that pits your mind against the matter of the other planet. Squares to your Mercury can toughen your mental agility and communication abilities when you recognize your inner inconsistencies.

Squares to Venus

My ability to interact with others is challenged and tested by the nature of the other planet.

Your capacity to form lasting relationships and your ability to create financial stability are undermined by the character of the planet that squares your Venus. You are challenged to own up to the internal issues and external squabbles that block your idea of bliss. Squares to your Venus can actually strengthen your sense of self-worth and your confidence in overcoming obstacles.

Squares to Mars

My actions and impatience are challenged and tested by the nature of the other planet.

Your capacity to take action disagrees with the personality of the other planet. The other planet dares and defies you to continue onward and upward without killing off a part of your soul. Sure, that sounds a bit violent and dramatic, and that's the point. Planets squaring your Mars get your blood up. The upside is that Mars squares boost your vitality and heighten your sex appeal.

Squares to Jupiter

My open-minded approach is challenged and tested by the nature of the other planet.

Your optimism and sense of opportunities are at odds with the energy of the other planet. You must acknowledge the stress between your philosophy and the nature of the other planet. In some cases, your sense of personal freedom is squelched by the other planet. Squares to Jupiter can also help you maximize your potential, as they encourage you to step out of your comfort zone and into your own great adventure.

Squares to Saturn

My capacity to achieve and find respect is challenged and tested by the nature of the other planet.

Your sense of accomplishment and ability to be respected are challenged by the identity of the other planet. Saturn squares are particularly difficult if you refuse to acknowledge the blocks and obstacles introduced by the other planet. Squares to Saturn can actually strengthen your capacity to succeed, as they drive you to reach for the pinnacle of success, personally and professionally.

Squares to Uranus

My independent nature is challenged and tested by the nature of the other planet.

Your individuality and capacity to see into the future are at odds with the energy of the other planet. You must acknowledge the anxiety between your own quirks and the nature of the other planet in order to renew your sense of logic and objectivity. Squares to Uranus often spark unusual situations and circumstances that challenge conventionality. Ultimately, a Uranus square challenges complacency in yourself and others and propels you to break old, outmoded patterns that no longer work in your spiritual path.

Squares to Neptune

My compassionate nature is challenged and tested by the nature of the other planet.

When Neptune conflicts with another planet in your chart, your desire to find the divine is blocked by the other planet. Your vision and idealism are at odds with this energy, and you are challenged to maintain your sensitivity as well as integrate the nature of the other planet. Squares to Neptune also act as a safeguard, helping you maintain a realistic view, rather than slipping into a fantasy world.

Squares to Pluto

My intense nature is challenged and tested by the nature of the other planet.

When Pluto challenges another planet in your chart, your power to shape your life is in disagreement with the nature of the other planet. Your strength and potency are at odds with the energy of the other planet. You must acknowledge the strain between your desire to transform your existence and the influences that block your sense of personal power. Ultimately, Pluto squares propel you to change your world, inside and out.

Quincunxes: Fateful Shifts

It's easy to stumble over the word quincunx, and much easier to fall on your fanny as you work with the quincunxes in your chart. That's because these clumsy combinations trick and trip you up to the point that you don't know whether you're coming or going.

Joan of Arc's chart (in the Introduction) shows a quincunx between her Mars and Uranus. Mars is in dedicated and virtuous Virgo, whereas wild and willful Uranus is in radical Aquarius. Her desire to act in a practical way (Mars in Virgo) was complicated by her rebellious ideas (Uranus in Aquarius). At times, Joan of Arc was incredibly devoted, and at other times she was a full-fledged rebel, instigating unrest in dramatic ways.

When you look at your own quincunxes, be gentle with yourself. Quincunxes reflect lifetimes of frustrated attempts to master specific issues. These complex and convoluted combinations point out the ragged edges and inconsistencies in your soul's code. If they were easy to manage and master, you would have figured them out by now. The good news is that these karmic connections between planets illustrate the odd twists and turns that direct you to your destiny, leading you ever nearer to the life you have imagined.

Quincunxes to the Sun

I must make peace between my personality and the energy of the other planet.

In past lives, you shied away from expressing yourself in the highest light, and now your ego and creative abilities are confronted by the unfamiliar attitudes of the other planet. The constant unrest and agitation reflected by quincunxes to your Sun describe your karmic quest. You will find peace when you integrate the enigmatic energy of the connecting planet and share your authentic self with others.

Quincunxes to the Moon

I must make peace between my emotions and the energy of the other planet.

Your spiritual history is marked by difficult challenges to your home and emotional security. Now, your understanding of your own needs and your sensitivity to others' needs are disputed by the strange nature of the other planet. The continuous turbulence reflected by quincunxes to your Moon defines an important aspect of your own soul's goal. You will discover serenity as you allow the essence of the connecting planet to expand your emotional understanding and expression.

Quincunxes to Mercury

I must make peace between my mindset and the energy of the other planet.

Your past lives included situations in which your ability to share your thoughts was hampered by either yourself or outside situations. Your soul hopes to change the pattern reflected by the quincunxes to Mercury in this lifetime and overcome your hesitancy to say what is really on your mind. As you incorporate the energy of the connecting planet, you will find greater confidence in your interaction, and a deep, lasting peace of mind.

Quincunxes to Venus

I must make peace between my values and the energy of the other planet.

In past lives, your values were out of sync with other aspects of your world. This had a detrimental effect on your finances, relationships, and self-worth. This time around, your soul intends to change things and shift the pattern of frustration inherent in the quincunxes to Venus. Ultimately, you are seeking to prevail in matters of the heart as well as the pocketbook. You will have great success when you encompass the nature of the connecting planet to assess your own worth in relationship to the world and everyone in it.

Quincunxes to Mars

I must make peace between my actions and the energy of the other planet.

Your karmic history is littered with unconquered battles and unsettled disputes. Now, your higher self hopes to take charge and move forward, regardless of past failures and foibles. The quincunxes to Mars reflect your uneasy truce with life and motivate you to stand up for yourself, even when it's not the popular thing to do. However, if you consider that the connecting planet is really part of your arsenal, you'll boost your self-confidence and put the odds in your favor, no matter what you're up against.

Quincunxes to Jupiter

I must make peace between my philosophy and the energy of the other planet.

Your spiritual history includes several lifetimes in which your own creed was out of vogue, or even downright illegal. As you move through this lifetime, you fear that one missed step could find you boiling in oil. Maybe not literally, but you are aware that stepping out of line with popular dogma is not a healthy choice. Quincunxes to Jupiter remind you that your soul longs for freedom of both thought and action and that your surprising ally in this quest is the acceptance and integration of the connecting planet.

Quincunxes to Saturn

I must make peace between my sense of responsibility and the energy of the other planet.

Your past lives were burdened by heavy responsibilities, and your progress and achievements were blocked by a multitude of obstacles. Now, it's only natural that you shy away from taking on certain responsibilities in this lifetime. Over and over again, you may be tempted to drop out and quit. But since your soul has every intention of overcoming these difficulties once and for all, the planets that quincunx your Saturn present the perfect approach to manifest success.

Quincunxes to Uranus

I must make peace between my desire for independence and the energy of the other planet.

In past lives, your individuality and ability to go your own way were challenged and obscured by events outside of your control. Now you hedge your bets and struggle with a defeatist belief that everything can be swept away in an instant. The quincunxes to Uranus constantly remind you that you are much more than a grain of sand tumbling in the cosmic surf and that you must plug into life's passions. It is the irritating energies of the connecting planets that draw your attention to the part of life that will help you shatter your fears and reshape your view of your own past, present, and potential.

Quincunxes to Neptune

I must make peace between my intuition and the energy of the other planet.

In past lives, you were inundated by sensitivity and sacrifice, and now you simply want to recede into your own little fantasyland. That may sound nice, but your higher self intends to dig deeper into your softer, gentler side. To further that cause, the quincunxes to your Neptune consistently create karmic situations in which you must listen to your intuition and pay attention to your inner vision. Fortunately, the connecting planets offer unusual and unlikely tools with which to navigate the ambiguous impressions of the unseen and unconscious worlds.

Quincunxes to Pluto

I must make peace between my sense of personal power and the energy of the other planet.

The power struggles and intrigue of your past lives have wearied your soul, and now you would like nothing more than to leave it all behind you. The quincunxes to Pluto remind you that you now have every intention of transcending the trickery and scams that scandalized your spiritual history. Rather than relying on old instincts, the connecting planet provides a potent impulse that transforms your life as well as your destiny.

Part Four Summary

1. Saturn.

   Saturn reminds you that you have a job to do and a karmic responsibility to do it well. If you're willing to do the work, Saturn rewards you with unshakable self-confidence as well as the respect and admiration of others.

   Saturn's sign: the nature of my karmic obligations and ambitions: _____

   _____

   _____

   Cosmic clue: _____

   Saturn's house: the part of my life burdened by extra responsibility: _____

   _____

   _____

   Cosmic clue: _____

   My own experiences: _____

   _____

   _____

2. Part of Karma.

   Use the sign and house of your Part of Karma to pinpoint the nature of the unfinished business and karmic tasks that can slow you down.

Part of Karma sign: how I can address
the unfinished business from past lives: _____

_____

_____

Cosmic clue: _____

Part of Karma house: where karmic issues
affect my life: _____

_____

_____

Cosmic clue: _____

My own experiences: _____

_____

_____

3. The South Node.
   The South Node's message contains talents and strengths from lives gone by and
   acts as a source of complacency in this lifetime.

   South Node sign: the instinct that I fall back on: _____

   _____

   _____

   Cosmic clue: _____

   South Node house: the part of my life that I fall back on: _____

   _____

   _____

   Cosmic clue: _____

   My own experiences: _____

   _____

   _____

4. Squares and quincunxes.

   The inner circle of your chart contains aspect lines that connect one planet to another. These lines tell you what kind of conversation is taking place between the two planets involved. For this exercise, look for lines with either a square (□) or quincunx (⛏). Not all planets will have squares and/or quincunxes. Once you note the squares and quincunxes contained in your chart, use this worksheet to better understand the cosmic conversations taking place. Here's a list of planetary keywords to help you on your way:

Planet	Glyph	Primary Impulse
Sun	☉	To create
Moon	☽	To respond, nurture
Mercury	☿	To learn, communicate
Venus	♀	To relate, acquire
Mars	♂	To act, fight
Jupiter	♃	To explore, expand
Saturn	♄	To be responsible
Uranus	♅	To break with tradition
Neptune	♆	To seek out the divine
Pluto	♇	To control your fate

Squares and quincunxes reflect the challenges you encounter as you move through your life. They also indicate internal conflicts and issues that must be resolved in this lifetime.

_____ squares _____.

My desire to _____ is challenged by my desire to _____.

_____ squares _____.

My desire to _____ is challenged by my desire to _____.

_____ squares _____.

My desire to _____ is challenged by my desire to _____.

_____ quincunxes _____.

My desire to _____ is out of sync with my desire to _____.

_____ quincunxes _____.

My desire to _____ is out of sync with my desire to _____.

_____ quincunxes _____.

My desire to _____ is out of sync with my desire to _____.

Part Five
Final Destination

If you don't know where you're headed, you'll end up somewhere else.

The highways and byways of your chart have supplied some pretty interesting insights into who you are and who you are becoming. There's one more indicator in your chart that sums up what this lifetime is about. It's called the Vertex, which is another name for the ultimate clue to your soul's intentions.

The Vertex (⊗) is a powerful indicator of your soul's main objective and includes important information about how others figure into your karmic quest. It is such a sacred part of your soul's code that it feels vulnerable and sensitive. Facing up to your vulnerabilities is challenging, but knowing your weak spots proves invaluable as you move forward on your spiritual path.

15
Vertex

The Ultimate Clue to Your Soul's Intentions

The sign in which your Vertex falls identifies the key instinct that your spirit is longing to express. The Vertex is always found on the relationship side of the chart, which includes the houses between the fourth- and tenth-house cusps. The house in which the Vertex falls defines the part of your life in which your own spiritual development is crucial. It also indicates the part of your life in which you receive support whenever you are honest and forthcoming about your own spiritual challenges.

Vertex in Aries

I am seeking courage and initiative.

At this point in your karmic journey, you are emerging from lifetimes of complacency and keeping the peace. Now, your soul yearns to be bold, brave, daring, and courageous. Taking charge is not a comfortable concept, but numerous conflicts and confrontations force you to rise to the challenge.

On the other hand, you are uneasy and unsure when it comes to being angry. It's difficult to find the perfect balance between acquiescence and aggression. As you move through life, you must act in your own self-interest, even when it isn't politically correct. You must define what you are fighting for and stay true to your convictions. When in doubt, avoid others who are selfish or impatient. Instead, you must consistently take action that serves your higher purpose.

If your Sun, North Node, Part of Fortune, or Jupiter is also in Aries, you have extra energy implementing your Aries Vertex. If your Moon, South Node, Part of Karma, or Saturn is also in Aries, this may be a quest that you have been working on for more than one lifetime.

Vertex in Taurus

I am seeking stability and perseverance.

You are emerging from lifetimes of constant upheaval and chaos. Now, your soul longs for peace, pleasure, stability, and security. If you mistake this desire for sheer materialism, the stuff and souvenirs you collect will provide little comfort. Rather than seeking the security of others, you must become self-sufficient and build your life upon a bedrock of self-worth.

Because you have been manipulated in past lives, you now look at life as an "own or be owned" proposition. That creed applies to relationships as well, and it is difficult to relate to others without wondering how much it will cost you in the end. Stick with your instincts, and avoid those who are possessive and controlling, especially if they undermine your self-confidence.

If your Sun, North Node, Part of Fortune, or Jupiter is also in Taurus, you have extra help in implementing your Vertex. If your Moon, South Node, Part of Karma, or Saturn is in Taurus, your Vertex may represent a quest that you have been working on for more than one lifetime.

Vertex in Gemini

I am seeking curiosity and flexibility.

You are emerging from lifetimes of swimming in the deep end of the intellectual ocean. Rather than trying to figure out the meaning of life, this lifetime is about paying attention to the bits and pieces of information that make a difference, like your spouse's birthday. Seriously, though, your soul is searching to reclaim the wild abandon and innocence of a young child chasing a butterfly through the garden. You are no longer searching for absolute answers. You simply want to delight in the myriad experiences along the way.

On the other hand, you are uneasy and unsure when it comes to being curious. It's difficult to find the perfect balance between asking questions and revealing that you don't know everything. In exposing your vulnerabilities, you can quickly identify those folks who are and aren't helpful to you. Remember that there are plenty of fish in the sea, so there's no reason to hang around anyone who mocks your mind.

The Sun, North Node, Part of Fortune, or Jupiter in Gemini provides a beneficial boost in mastering your Vertex in Gemini. However, the Moon, South Node, Part of Karma, or Saturn in Gemini reflects conflicts that challenge your Vertex throughout your life.

Vertex in Cancer or in the Fourth House

I am seeking emotional sensitivity.

Your Vertex in Cancer suggests that you have built your past lives on blind ambition. Now, you are searching for the gentle ebb and flow of unconditional love and acceptance. Lifetimes of achievement have taught you that true love is rare. Your soul yearns to establish a foundation of kindness and tenderness in this lifetime, but you feel ill at ease in emotional waters.

Encounters with others who are harsh and uncaring will corner you and ultimately force you to seek refuge in the long-dormant sensitivity of your own soul. On the other hand, you are uneasy and unsure when it comes to reaching out and understanding the emotional cues of others. Relationships will always lead you into uncharted emotional territory, and you will need to rely on your own savvy to avoid those who exploit your lack of emotional confidence.

The Sun, North Node, Part of Fortune, or Jupiter in Cancer supports the emotional nature of your Vertex in Cancer. The Moon, South Node, Part of Karma, or Saturn in Cancer creates obstacles and suggests that the emotional intelligence of Cancer is a quest that you have been working toward for more than one lifetime.

Vertex in Leo or in the Fifth House

I am seeking passion and generosity.

At this point in your own karmic journey, you are emerging from lifetimes of keeping your distance and avoiding intimacy. Now, your soul longs to be loving, passionate, and fully engaged, especially in relationships. You would just love to be loved, but reaching out does not come naturally. Over and over again, you are left feeling like the odd man out and think that you must do outrageous things to attract attention.

Once you do attract someone, it's awkward finding the right mix of connection and independence within the relationship. If you focus on what you are creating in the relationship, you will be more relaxed. Even then, you must fix your mind and body firmly in the present and avoid the temptation to retreat to living in your head.

The Sun, North Node, Part of Fortune, or Jupiter in Leo provides additional support as your work with your Vertex. The Moon, South Node, Part of Karma, or Saturn in Leo implies that this is a quest that you have been working on for more than one lifetime.

Vertex in Virgo or in the Sixth House

I am seeking order and dedication.

You have spent lifetimes searching for the divine while living in the protected haven of a convent or monastery. Now, your soul yearns to combine the vision and illumination of those lifetimes with the reality of daily duties. Your spirit is hungry for physical connection—to the earth, to others, and even to your own physical existence. As you pursue that goal, you are frequently challenged to stay grounded and to recognize that life is perfect as it is.

On the other hand, you are uncertain and ambivalent when it comes to dealing with the details of life in progress, especially in your relationships with others. Since you've spent lifetimes communing with the gods, meeting up with mortals can seem like a letdown. However, your Vertex in Virgo suggests that being connected to others can actually lead you to heaven on earth.

The Sun, North Node, Part of Fortune, or Jupiter in Virgo provides help in perfecting your Virgo mission. The Moon, South Node, Part of Karma, or Saturn in Virgo signifies that you have been working on this quest for more than one lifetime.

Vertex in Libra or in the Seventh House

I am seeking balance and harmony.

Your spiritual history is founded on lifetimes of being your own person and looking out for number one. At the end of all that action, you longed for peace and quiet and a gentle partner to accompany you down life's path. Now that you think of it, some of those social graces and diplomacy might come in handy, as well. Despite these desires, you are constantly forced into confrontations where peace seems like a distant dream. It would be easy to come out swinging, but you are well aware that you signed up to create harmony in this lifetime, even at the eleventh hour. You must preserve your identity, both in and out of relationships, but you are uneasy and unsure when it comes to negotiations. It is a challenge to find the perfect balance between your strong sense of self and the delicacy required to understand another person.

The Sun, North Node, Part of Fortune, or Jupiter in Libra gives power to your Vertex. The Moon, South Node, Part of Karma, or Saturn in Libra suggests that this is a quest that you have been working on for more than one lifetime.

Vertex in Scorpio or in the Eighth House

I am seeking intensity and control.

Your Vertex in Scorpio indicates that you have spent lifetimes preserving the status quo. Now, you crave change and long to transform the placid predictability that numbed your mind in past lives, and you frequently find yourself in circumstances that force you to start from scratch.

You are uneasy in the role you have chosen in this lifetime; creating chaos out of order is never the popular thing to do. The Vertex in Scorpio attracts those who are fascinated with the strength that seems to run through you. However, it is these same relationships that force you to find the delicate balance between being in control and being controlling. Ultimately, you must choose those people who understand and support your soul purpose to master your own power.

The Sun, North Node, Part of Fortune, or Jupiter in Scorpio empowers your Vertex in Scorpio. The Moon, South Node, Part of Karma, or Saturn in Scorpio indicates that this is a repeating theme from past lives.

Vertex in Sagittarius or in the Ninth House

I am seeking freedom and adventure.

At this point in your own karmic journey, you are emerging from lifetimes of dabbling in any number of interesting pursuits. Now, you're ready to focus on finding the pattern behind all of your comings and goings. That's not to say that you never let your curiosity get the better of you, but you frequently find yourself in situations where you must adopt a more enlightened view and share it with others. You would much rather ask questions than answer them, and it's hard to find the balance between too much information and not enough insight. Over and over again, the Vertex in Sagittarius reminds you that information without application is so much wasted effort.

The Sun, North Node, Part of Fortune, or Jupiter in Sagittarius provides additional inspiration as you integrate the lessons of your Vertex. The Moon, South Node, Part of Karma, or Saturn in Sagittarius suggests that you have been working on this particular quest for more than one lifetime.

Vertex in Capricorn

I am seeking accomplishment and respect.

Your spiritual history is filled with lifetimes where you served as the primary source of nurturing to everyone around you. Now you're hungering to go out into the big, wide world and try your hand at a different kind of undertaking.

As you work with your Vertex in Capricorn, you often lack the confidence to move forward and make things happen. Relationships quickly engage your emotions, and to succeed, you must draw appropriate boundaries and listen to your own wisdom, despite the cries of those around you. It is especially important to associate with people who are emotionally healthy and capable of meeting their own needs.

The Sun, North Node, Part of Fortune, or Jupiter in Capricorn forms a solid foundation on which to understand your Vertex. The Moon, South Node, Part of Karma, or Saturn in Capricorn represents that this is a quest you have been working on for more than one lifetime.

Vertex in Aquarius

I am seeking autonomy and individuality.

At this point in your own karmic journey, you are emerging from lifetimes of putting on a show for others. Now, your soul yearns to break out of the gilded cage of fame and fortune and plan for a future where you have the freedom to do as you please. Living life unscripted is harder than you ever imagined, and it's easy to let your vanity get the best of you. It's always difficult to do your own thing and not worry about political correctness or public opinion. Relationships throw a harsh light on your intentions whenever you sacrifice your independence for a few cheap thrills. However, when you actively seek out partners who are happy with their own quirks and eccentricities, you'll find the acceptance you are searching for.

The Sun, North Node, Part of Fortune, or Jupiter in Aquarius sheds light on your Vertex. The Moon, South Node, Part of Karma, or Saturn in Aquarius suggests that you have been dealing with this issue for more than one lifetime.

Vertex in Pisces

I am seeking intuition and compassion.

Your spiritual history is marked by lifetimes of arduous work and service. To say you're ready for a vacation is an understatement. Now, your soul longs for a kinder, gentler existence in which fairy tales do come true. But just like a busy executive on vacation, it's hard to relax and get into the rhythm of life without a to-do list.

That's not to say that your dance card isn't full. It is. However, you often find yourself in situations in which you must create an island of peace and quiet, despite others' agendas and expectations. Choosing partners who understand what a leap of faith it is for you to listen to your intuition will make a big difference in your spiritual satisfaction.

The Sun, North Node, Part of Fortune, or Jupiter in Pisces provides some extra blessings when it comes to understanding your Vertex. The Moon, South Node, Part of Karma, or Saturn in Pisces hints that you have been working on this mission for more than one lifetime.

Part Five Summary

The Vertex is a powerful indicator of your soul's highest objective in this lifetime and includes important information about how others figure into your karmic quest. Use this worksheet to make note of your own Vertex placement by sign and house. You'll also want to identify other points that fall in the same sign, as they may challenge your Vertex or provide assistance.

Vertex sign: the key energy my soul is longing to express: _____

_____

_____

Cosmic clue: _____

My Vertex is supported by any of the following points in the same sign:
Sun, North Node, Part of Fortune, or Jupiter: _____

_____

_____

My Vertex is challenged by any of the following points in the same sign:
Moon, South Node, Part of Karma, or Saturn: _____

_____

_____

Vertex house: where I am vulnerable: _____

_____

_____

Cosmic clue: _____

My own experiences: _____

_____

_____

A Final Word

As you apply these tools to gain insight into your own spiritual journey, as well as the paths of your friends and lovers, keep the following in mind:

- Human beings are complex combinations of differing needs and desires. Your own internal conflicts are reflected in different parts of the chart. Contradictions reflect the fact that your own soul purpose is comprised of many different issues, some of which are easily understood and others which are quite complicated.

- Some themes repeat. The unique combination of factors used in this book serves to verify and clarify specific issues in your spiritual path. The more often an issue shows up, the more pertinent it is in your journey.

- Not every item is relevant to your life today. Thankfully, you don't have to work on all of your karmic issues all of the time. Some issues will surface, be resolved, and recede, while others will be continually present. The good news is that the information contained in this book will become more meaningful each time you use it.

Appendix 1
Eclipse Tables

To find the Solar and Lunar Eclipses that occurred prior to your birth, follow these easy steps:

1. Find your birth year in the following list.

2. Find the dates of the two eclipses that fall immediately before your birthday. It's possible that one or both of your eclipses might actually fall in the year prior to your birth. Note the eclipse types and zodiac signs of each eclipse.

3. If the two eclipses prior to your birth are Lunar, both eclipses will apply to your spiritual path. To determine your Solar Eclipse, look for the next Solar Eclipse that falls prior to your birth.

4. If the two eclipses prior to your birth are Solar, both eclipses will apply to your spiritual path. To determine your Lunar Eclipse, look for the next Lunar Eclipse that falls prior to your birth.

5. The eclipse times are listed in Greenwich Mean Time. If you were born in a different time zone within one day of an eclipse, your best bet is to consult a professional astrologer to determine whether you were born before or after the eclipse.

6. You will need to refer to your birth chart to determine the house placement of each eclipse. The signs proceed in counterclockwise order around the chart. Find the house cusp that is the same sign as your prenatal Solar or Lunar Eclipse. Next, compare the degree of the eclipse with the degree of the house cusp. If the degree of the eclipse is smaller than the degree on the house cusp, the eclipse falls in the previous house. If the degree of the eclipse is greater than the degree on the house cusp, the eclipse falls in that house.

For example, if you were born on February 20, 1953, your prenatal Solar Eclipse is 25° Aquarius and your prenatal Lunar Eclipse is 9° Leo. If your second-house cusp is 14° Aquarius, the Solar Eclipse will fall in your second house. If your eighth-house cusp is 14° Leo, your Lunar Eclipse will fall in your seventh house.

Examples

Example 1

- Birth date: October 10, 1976

- Find your birth year. Notice that your birthday falls *before* the eclipse on October 22, so your eclipses would be the two preceding eclipses on May 13 and April 29. Make a note on your chart that your prenatal Lunar Eclipse is Scorpio and your prenatal Solar Eclipse is Taurus.

Apr 29, 1976	04:23	Solar Eclipse	09° Taurus 14'
May 13, 1976	13:53	Lunar Eclipse	23° Scorpio 10'
Oct 22, 1976	23:13	Solar Eclipse	29° Libra 56'
Nov 6, 1976	17:00	Lunar Eclipse	14° Taurus 40'

Example 2

- Birth date: January 31, 1953

- Find your birth year. Notice that your birthday falls before the second eclipse of 1953 on February 13, so you must refer to the eclipses of the prior year. Your eclipses fall on January 29, 1953, and August 20, 1952. Make a note on your chart that your prenatal Lunar Eclipse is Leo and your prenatal Solar Eclipse is also Leo.

Aug 20, 1952	09:12	Solar Eclipse	27° Leo 31'
Jan 29, 1953	17:47	Lunar Eclipse	09° Leo 48'
Feb 13, 1953	18:58	Solar Eclipse	25° Aquarius 03'
Jul 10, 1953	20:43	Solar Eclipse	18° Cancer 30'
Jul 26, 1953	06:21	Lunar Eclipse	03° Aquarius 12'
Aug 9, 1953	09:55	Solar Eclipse	16° Leo 45'

Example 3

- Birth date: July 4, 1982
- Find your birth year. Notice that your birthday falls before the eclipse on July 6. Since the two eclipses prior to your birth on June 21 and January 24 are both Solar Eclipses, you must refer to the third eclipse prior to your birth to determine your Lunar Eclipse. Make a note on your chart that your prenatal Lunar Eclipse is Cancer and your prenatal Solar Eclipses are Aquarius and Gemini.

Jan 9, 1982	13:56	Lunar Eclipse	19° Cancer 14'
Jan 24, 1982	22:41	Solar Eclipse	04° Aquarius 53'
Jun 21, 1982	06:03	Solar Eclipse	29° Gemini 47'
Jul 6, 1982	01:30	Lunar Eclipse	13° Capricorn 55'
Jul 20, 1982	12:44	Solar Eclipse	27° Cancer 43'
Dec 15, 1982	03:31	Solar Eclipse	23° Sagittarius 05'
Dec 30, 1982	05:28	Lunar Eclipse	08° Cancer 26'

Eclipses 1920-2010[1]

	Date	Time	Type	Zodiac Position
1920	May 2, 1920	19:51	Lunar Eclipse	12° Scorpio 19'
	May 18, 1920	00:14	Solar Eclipse	26° Taurus 59'
	Oct 27, 1920	08:11	Lunar Eclipse	03° Taurus 52'
	Nov 10, 1920	09:51	Solar Eclipse	17° Scorpio 58'

Date	Time	Type	Zodiac Position
Apr 8, 1921	03:15	Solar Eclipse	18° Aries 00'
Apr 22, 1921	01:43	Lunar Eclipse	01° Scorpio 38'
Oct 1, 1921	06:35	Solar Eclipse	07° Libra 47'
Oct 16, 1921	16:53	Lunar Eclipse	23° Aries 02'
Mar 13, 1922	05:27	Lunar Eclipse	22° Virgo 07'
Mar 28, 1922	07:05	Solar Eclipse	07° Aries 04'
Apr 11, 1922	14:31	Lunar Eclipse	21° Libra 10'
Sep 20, 1922	22:40	Solar Eclipse	27° Virgo 25'
Oct 5, 1922	18:42	Lunar Eclipse	11° Aries 59'
Mar 2, 1923	21:32	Lunar Eclipse	11° Virgo 33'
Mar 17, 1923	06:45	Solar Eclipse	25° Pisces 55'
Aug 26, 1923	04:39	Lunar Eclipse	02° Pisces 10'
Sep 10, 1923	14:47	Solar Eclipse	17° Virgo 06'
Feb 20, 1924	10:08	Lunar Eclipse	00° Virgo 46'
Mar 5, 1924	09:44	Solar Eclipse	14° Pisces 49'
Jul 31, 1924	13:57	Solar Eclipse	08° Leo 17'
Aug 14, 1924	14:20	Lunar Eclipse	21° Aquarius 43'
Aug 30, 1924	02:23	Solar Eclipse	06° Virgo 40'
Jan 24, 1925	08:53	Solar Eclipse	04° Aquarius 08'
Feb 8, 1925	15:41	Lunar Eclipse	19° Leo 39'
Jul 20, 1925	15:47	Solar Eclipse	27° Cancer 37'
Aug 4, 1925	05:53	Lunar Eclipse	11° Aquarius 34'
Jan 14, 1926	00:37	Solar Eclipse	23° Capricorn 21'
Jan 28, 1926	15:20	Lunar Eclipse	08° Leo 13'
Jun 25, 1926	15:24	Lunar Eclipse	03° Capricorn 32'
Jul 9, 1926	17:05	Solar Eclipse	16° Cancer 57'
Jul 24, 1926	23:00	Lunar Eclipse	01° Aquarius 30'
Dec 19, 1926	00:20	Lunar Eclipse	26° Gemini 36'

Date	Time	Type	Zodiac Position
Jan 3, 1927	14:22	Solar Eclipse	12° Capricorn 29'
Jun 15, 1927	02:24	Lunar Eclipse	23° Sagittarius 15'
Jun 29, 1927	00:22	Solar Eclipse	06° Cancer 31'
Dec 8, 1927	11:35	Lunar Eclipse	15° Gemini 38'
Dec 23, 1927	21:58	Solar Eclipse	01° Capricorn 21'
May 19, 1928	07:23	Solar Eclipse	28° Taurus 18'
Jun 3, 1928	06:09	Lunar Eclipse	12° Sagittarius 39'
Jun 17, 1928	14:26	Solar Eclipse	26° Gemini 21'
Nov 12, 1928	03:48	Solar Eclipse	19° Scorpio 47'
Nov 27, 1928	03:00	Lunar Eclipse	04° Gemini 53'
May 9, 1929	00:10	Solar Eclipse	18° Taurus 07'
May 23, 1929	06:36	Lunar Eclipse	01° Sagittarius 52'
Nov 1, 1929	06:04	Solar Eclipse	08° Scorpio 35'
Nov 16, 1929	18:02	Lunar Eclipse	24° Taurus 10'

1930

Date	Time	Type	Zodiac Position
Apr 12, 1930	23:59	Lunar Eclipse	22° Libra 35'
Apr 28, 1930	13:03	Solar Eclipse	07° Taurus 45'
Oct 7, 1930	13:07	Lunar Eclipse	13° Aries 47'
Oct 21, 1930	15:43	Solar Eclipse	27° Libra 46'
Apr 2, 1931	14:07	Lunar Eclipse	12° Libra 07'
Apr 17, 1931	18:45	Solar Eclipse	27° Aries 02'
Sep 11, 1931	22:41	Solar Eclipse	18° Virgo 28'
Sep 26, 1931	13:48	Lunar Eclipse	02° Aries 45'
Oct 11, 1931	06:55	Solar Eclipse	17° Libra 15'
Mar 7, 1932	01:55	Solar Eclipse	16° Pisces 33'
Mar 22, 1932	06:32	Lunar Eclipse	01° Libra 41'
Aug 31, 1932	14:03	Solar Eclipse	08° Virgo 10'
Sep 14, 1932	15:00	Lunar Eclipse	21° Pisces 49'

Date	Time	Type	Zodiac Position
Feb 10, 1933	07:17	Lunar Eclipse	21° Leo 23'
Feb 24, 1933	06:45	Solar Eclipse	05° Pisces 29'
Mar 11, 1933	20:32	Lunar Eclipse	21° Virgo 05'
Aug 5, 1933	13:46	Lunar Eclipse	12° Aquarius 54'
Aug 20, 1933	23:48	Solar Eclipse	27° Leo 42'
Sep 3, 1933	22:52	Lunar Eclipse	11° Pisces 12'
Jan 30, 1934	10:41	Lunar Eclipse	10° Leo 07'
Feb 13, 1934	18:38	Solar Eclipse	24° Aquarius 38'
Jul 26, 1934	06:14	Lunar Eclipse	02° Aquarius 48'
Aug 10, 1934	02:37	Solar Eclipse	17° Leo 01'
Jan 4, 1935	23:34	Solar Eclipse	13° Capricorn 58'
Jan 19, 1935	09:46	Lunar Eclipse	28° Cancer 39'
Feb 3, 1935	10:15	Solar Eclipse	13° Aquarius 55'
Jun 30, 1935	13:59	Solar Eclipse	08° Cancer 05'
Jul 15, 1935	22:59	Lunar Eclipse	22° Capricorn 45'
Jul 30, 1935	03:15	Solar Eclipse	06° Leo 17'
Dec 25, 1935	11:59	Solar Eclipse	03° Capricorn 02'
Jan 8, 1936	12:10	Lunar Eclipse	17° Cancer 19'
Jun 18, 1936	23:19	Solar Eclipse	27° Gemini 44'
Jul 4, 1936	11:25	Lunar Eclipse	12° Capricorn 31'
Dec 13, 1936	17:27	Solar Eclipse	21° Sagittarius 49'
Dec 27, 1936	21:48	Lunar Eclipse	06° Cancer 15'
May 25, 1937	01:51	Lunar Eclipse	03° Sagittarius 41'
Jun 8, 1937	14:41	Solar Eclipse	17° Gemini 36'
Nov 18, 1937	02:18	Lunar Eclipse	25° Taurus 35'
Dec 2, 1937	17:05	Solar Eclipse	10° Sagittarius 22'
May 14, 1938	02:43	Lunar Eclipse	22° Scorpio 54'
May 29, 1938	07:50	Solar Eclipse	07° Gemini 31'
Nov 7, 1938	16:26	Lunar Eclipse	14° Taurus 52'
Nov 21, 1938	17:51	Solar Eclipse	29° Scorpio 01'

Date	Time	Type	Zodiac Position
Apr 19, 1939	10:44	Solar Eclipse	28° Aries 44'
May 3, 1939	09:11	Lunar Eclipse	12° Scorpio 17'
Oct 12, 1939	14:39	Solar Eclipse	18° Libra 37'
Oct 28, 1939	00:35	Lunar Eclipse	03° Taurus 56'
1940 Mar 23, 1940	13:48	Lunar Eclipse	03° Libra 02'
Apr 7, 1940	14:20	Solar Eclipse	17° Aries 52'
Apr 21, 1940	22:26	Lunar Eclipse	01° Scorpio 54'
Oct 1, 1940	06:44	Solar Eclipse	08° Libra 11'
Oct 16, 1940	02:01	Lunar Eclipse	22° Aries 48'
Mar 13, 1941	05:54	Lunar Eclipse	22° Virgo 31'
Mar 27, 1941	14:07	Solar Eclipse	06° Aries 46'
Sep 5, 1941	11:46	Lunar Eclipse	12° Pisces 45'
Sep 20, 1941	22:33	Solar Eclipse	27° Virgo 48'
Mar 2, 1942	18:21	Lunar Eclipse	11° Virgo 48'
Mar 16, 1942	17:37	Solar Eclipse	25° Pisces 45'
Aug 11, 1942	20:44	Solar Eclipse	18° Leo 46'
Aug 25, 1942	21:47	Lunar Eclipse	02° Pisces 17'
Sep 10, 1942	09:39	Solar Eclipse	17° Virgo 17'
Feb 4, 1943	17:37	Solar Eclipse	15° Aquarius 18'
Feb 19, 1943	23:37	Lunar Eclipse	00° Virgo 43'
Jul 31, 1943	22:16	Solar Eclipse	08° Leo 03'
Aug 15, 1943	13:28	Lunar Eclipse	22° Aquarius 05'
Jan 25, 1944	09:25	Solar Eclipse	04° Aquarius 33'
Feb 8, 1944	23:14	Lunar Eclipse	19° Leo 20'
Jul 5, 1944	22:40	Lunar Eclipse	13° Capricorn 58'
Jul 19, 1944	23:42	Solar Eclipse	27° Cancer 22'
Aug 4, 1944	06:25	Lunar Eclipse	11° Aquarius 58'
Dec 29, 1944	08:48	Lunar Eclipse	07° Cancer 48'

Date	Time	Type	Zodiac Position
Jan 13, 1945	23:01	Solar Eclipse	23° Capricorn 41'
Jun 25, 1945	09:13	Lunar Eclipse	03° Capricorn 40'
Jul 9, 1945	07:26	Solar Eclipse	16° Cancer 57'
Dec 18, 1945	20:19	Lunar Eclipse	26° Gemini 50'
Jan 3, 1946	06:15	Solar Eclipse	12° Capricorn 32'
May 30, 1946	15:00	Solar Eclipse	08° Gemini 49'
Jun 14, 1946	12:39	Lunar Eclipse	23° Sagittarius 05'
Jun 28, 1946	21:52	Solar Eclipse	06° Cancer 48'
Nov 23, 1946	11:37	Solar Eclipse	00° Sagittarius 50'
Dec 8, 1946	11:48	Lunar Eclipse	16° Gemini 03'
May 20, 1947	07:47	Solar Eclipse	28° Taurus 42'
Jun 3, 1947	13:14	Lunar Eclipse	12° Sagittarius 21'
Nov 12, 1947	14:04	Solar Eclipse	19° Scorpio 36'
Nov 28, 1947	02:34	Lunar Eclipse	05° Gemini 16'
Apr 23, 1948	07:39	Lunar Eclipse	03° Scorpio 18'
May 8, 1948	20:26	Solar Eclipse	18° Taurus 22'
Oct 17, 1948	20:35	Lunar Eclipse	24° Aries 37'
Oct 31, 1948	23:59	Solar Eclipse	08° Scorpio 44'
Apr 12, 1949	22:11	Lunar Eclipse	22° Libra 54'
Apr 28, 1949	01:48	Solar Eclipse	07° Taurus 41'
Oct 6, 1949	20:56	Lunar Eclipse	13° Aries 31'
Oct 21, 1949	15:12	Solar Eclipse	28° Libra 08'
1950 Mar 18, 1950	09:32	Solar Eclipse	27° Pisces 28'
Apr 2, 1950	14:44	Lunar Eclipse	12° Libra 32'
Sep 11, 1950	21:38	Solar Eclipse	18° Virgo 49'
Sep 25, 1950	22:17	Lunar Eclipse	02° Aries 31'
Feb 21, 1951	15:29	Lunar Eclipse	02° Virgo 27'
Mar 7, 1951	14:53	Solar Eclipse	16° Pisces 29'

Date	Time	Type	Zodiac Position
Mar 23, 1951	04:37	Lunar Eclipse	02° Libra 00'
Aug 16, 1951	21:13	Lunar Eclipse	23° Aquarius 25'
Sep 1, 1951	06:51	Solar Eclipse	08° Virgo 17'
Sep 15, 1951	06:27	Lunar Eclipse	21° Pisces 51'
Feb 10, 1952	18:39	Lunar Eclipse	21° Leo 14'
Feb 25, 1952	03:11	Solar Eclipse	05° Pisces 43'
Aug 5, 1952	13:46	Lunar Eclipse	13° Aquarius 18'
Aug 20, 1952	09:12	Solar Eclipse	27° Leo 31'
Jan 29, 1953	17:47	Lunar Eclipse	09° Leo 48'
Feb 13, 1953	18:58	Solar Eclipse	25° Aquarius 03'
Jul 10, 1953	20:43	Solar Eclipse	18° Cancer 30'
Jul 26, 1953	06:21	Lunar Eclipse	03° Aquarius 12'
Aug 9, 1953	09:55	Solar Eclipse	16° Leo 45'
Jan 4, 1954	20:31	Solar Eclipse	14° Capricorn 14'
Jan 18, 1954	20:32	Lunar Eclipse	28° Cancer 29'
Jun 30, 1954	06:32	Solar Eclipse	08° Cancer 10'
Jul 15, 1954	18:20	Lunar Eclipse	22° Capricorn 57'
Dec 25, 1954	01:36	Solar Eclipse	02° Capricorn 59'
Jan 8, 1955	06:33	Lunar Eclipse	17° Cancer 28'
Jun 5, 1955	08:23	Lunar Eclipse	14° Sagittarius 09'
Jun 19, 1955	22:09	Solar Eclipse	28° Gemini 05'
Nov 29, 1955	10:59	Lunar Eclipse	06° Gemini 42'
Dec 14, 1955	01:01	Solar Eclipse	21° Sagittarius 31'
May 24, 1956	09:31	Lunar Eclipse	03° Sagittarius 25'
Jun 8, 1956	15:20	Solar Eclipse	18° Gemini 01'
Nov 18, 1956	00:47	Lunar Eclipse	25° Taurus 55'
Dec 2, 1956	01:59	Solar Eclipse	10° Sagittarius 08'

Date	Time	Type	Zodiac Position
Apr 29, 1957	18:04	Solar Eclipse	09° Taurus 23'
May 13, 1957	16:30	Lunar Eclipse	22° Scorpio 52'
Oct 22, 1957	22:52	Solar Eclipse	29° Libra 31'
Nov 7, 1957	08:26	Lunar Eclipse	14° Taurus 55'
Apr 3, 1958	22:00	Lunar Eclipse	13° Libra 53'
Apr 18, 1958	21:26	Solar Eclipse	28° Aries 35'
May 3, 1958	06:12	Lunar Eclipse	12° Scorpio 33'
Oct 12, 1958	14:54	Solar Eclipse	19° Libra 01'
Oct 27, 1958	09:26	Lunar Eclipse	03° Taurus 42'
Mar 24, 1959	14:11	Lunar Eclipse	03° Libra 26'
Apr 7, 1959	21:24	Solar Eclipse	17° Aries 33'
Sep 16, 1959	19:03	Lunar Eclipse	23° Pisces 24'
Oct 2, 1959	06:25	Solar Eclipse	08° Libra 34'

1960

Date	Time	Type	Zodiac Position
Mar 13, 1960	02:27	Lunar Eclipse	22° Virgo 47'
Mar 27, 1960	01:25	Solar Eclipse	06° Aries 38'
Sep 5, 1960	05:20	Lunar Eclipse	12° Pisces 53'
Sep 20, 1960	16:59	Solar Eclipse	27° Virgo 58'
Feb 15, 1961	02:19	Solar Eclipse	26° Aquarius 26'
Mar 2, 1961	07:28	Lunar Eclipse	11° Virgo 44'
Aug 11, 1961	04:46	Solar Eclipse	18° Leo 31'
Aug 25, 1961	21:08	Lunar Eclipse	02° Pisces 39'
Feb 4, 1962	18:11	Solar Eclipse	15° Aquarius 43'
Feb 19, 1962	07:03	Lunar Eclipse	00° Virgo 25'
Jul 17, 1962	05:53	Lunar Eclipse	24° Capricorn 25'
Jul 31, 1962	06:24	Solar Eclipse	07° Leo 49'
Aug 15, 1962	13:57	Lunar Eclipse	22° Aquarius 30'
Jan 9, 1963	17:19	Lunar Eclipse	18° Cancer 59'
Jan 25, 1963	07:37	Solar Eclipse	04° Aquarius 52'

Date	Time	Type	Zodiac Position
Jul 6, 1963	16:01	Lunar Eclipse	14° Capricorn 06'
Jul 20, 1963	14:36	Solar Eclipse	27° Cancer 24'
Dec 30, 1963	05:06	Lunar Eclipse	08° Cancer 02'
Jan 14, 1964	14:30	Solar Eclipse	23° Capricorn 43'
Jun 9, 1964	22:34	Solar Eclipse	19° Gemini 19'
Jun 24, 1964	19:06	Lunar Eclipse	03° Capricorn 30'
Jul 9, 1964	05:16	Solar Eclipse	17° Cancer 15'
Dec 3, 1964	19:31	Solar Eclipse	11° Sagittarius 56'
Dec 18, 1964	20:37	Lunar Eclipse	27° Gemini 14'
May 30, 1965	15:17	Solar Eclipse	09° Gemini 13'
Jun 13, 1965	19:48	Lunar Eclipse	22° Sagittarius 48'
Nov 22, 1965	22:14	Solar Eclipse	00° Sagittarius 40'
Dec 8, 1965	11:09	Lunar Eclipse	16° Gemini 25'
May 4, 1966	15:11	Lunar Eclipse	13° Scorpio 56'
May 20, 1966	03:37	Solar Eclipse	28° Taurus 55'
Oct 29, 1966	04:11	Lunar Eclipse	05° Taurus 32'
Nov 12, 1966	08:22	Solar Eclipse	19° Scorpio 45'
Apr 24, 1967	06:06	Lunar Eclipse	03° Scorpio 37'
May 9, 1967	08:42	Solar Eclipse	18° Taurus 17'
Oct 18, 1967	04:15	Lunar Eclipse	24° Aries 21'
Nov 1, 1967	23:38	Solar Eclipse	09° Scorpio 07'
Mar 28, 1968	17:00	Solar Eclipse	08° Aries 20'
Apr 12, 1968	22:46	Lunar Eclipse	23° Libra 19'
Sep 22, 1968	05:17	Solar Eclipse	29° Virgo 30'
Oct 6, 1968	05:42	Lunar Eclipse	13° Aries 17'
Mar 17, 1969	22:53	Solar Eclipse	27° Pisces 25'
Apr 2, 1969	12:32	Lunar Eclipse	12° Libra 50'

Date	Time	Type	Zodiac Position
Aug 27, 1969	04:48	Lunar Eclipse	03° Pisces 59'
Sep 11, 1969	13:58	Solar Eclipse	18° Virgo 53'
Sep 25, 1969	14:10	Lunar Eclipse	02° Aries 34'
1970 Feb 21, 1970	02:29	Lunar Eclipse	02° Virgo 18'
Mar 7, 1970	11:37	Solar Eclipse	16° Pisces 44'
Aug 16, 1970	21:22	Lunar Eclipse	23° Aquarius 49'
Aug 31, 1970	15:55	Solar Eclipse	08° Virgo 04'
Feb 10, 1971	01:45	Lunar Eclipse	20° Leo 55'
Feb 25, 1971	03:36	Solar Eclipse	06° Pisces 08'
Jul 22, 1971	03:31	Solar Eclipse	28° Cancer 56'
Aug 6, 1971	13:43	Lunar Eclipse	13° Aquarius 41'
Aug 20, 1971	16:39	Solar Eclipse	27° Leo 15'
Jan 16, 1972	05:03	Solar Eclipse	25° Capricorn 25'
Jan 30, 1972	04:52	Lunar Eclipse	09° Leo 39'
Jul 10, 1972	13:46	Solar Eclipse	18° Cancer 37'
Jul 26, 1972	01:16	Lunar Eclipse	03° Aquarius 23'
Jan 4, 1973	09:45	Solar Eclipse	14° Capricorn 10'
Jan 18, 1973	15:17	Lunar Eclipse	28° Cancer 40'
Jun 15, 1973	14:49	Lunar Eclipse	24° Sagittarius 35'
Jun 30, 1973	05:37	Solar Eclipse	08° Cancer 32'
Jul 15, 1973	05:38	Lunar Eclipse	22° Capricorn 50'
Dec 9, 1973	19:43	Lunar Eclipse	17° Gemini 52'
Dec 24, 1973	09:01	Solar Eclipse	02° Capricorn 40'
Jun 4, 1974	16:15	Lunar Eclipse	13° Sagittarius 54'
Jun 19, 1974	22:47	Solar Eclipse	28° Gemini 30'
Nov 29, 1974	09:12	Lunar Eclipse	07° Gemini 01'
Dec 13, 1974	10:12	Solar Eclipse	21° Sagittarius 16'

Date	Time	Type	Zodiac Position
May 11, 1975	01:17	Solar Eclipse	20° Taurus 00'
May 24, 1975	23:48	Lunar Eclipse	03° Sagittarius 25'
Nov 3, 1975	07:14	Solar Eclipse	10° Scorpio 30'
Nov 18, 1975	16:22	Lunar Eclipse	25° Taurus 57'
Apr 29, 1976	04:23	Solar Eclipse	09° Taurus 14'
May 13, 1976	13:53	Lunar Eclipse	23° Scorpio 10'
Oct 22, 1976	23:13	Solar Eclipse	29° Libra 56'
Nov 6, 1976	17:00	Lunar Eclipse	14° Taurus 40'
Apr 3, 1977	22:17	Lunar Eclipse	14° Libra 17'
Apr 18, 1977	04:30	Solar Eclipse	28° Aries 16'
Sep 27, 1977	02:28	Lunar Eclipse	04° Aries 07'
Oct 12, 1977	14:26	Solar Eclipse	19° Libra 24'
Mar 24, 1978	10:21	Lunar Eclipse	03° Libra 40'
Apr 7, 1978	09:02	Solar Eclipse	17° Aries 26'
Sep 16, 1978	13:04	Lunar Eclipse	23° Pisces 33'
Oct 2, 1978	00:28	Solar Eclipse	08° Libra 43'
Feb 26, 1979	10:53	Solar Eclipse	07° Pisces 30'
Mar 13, 1979	15:07	Lunar Eclipse	22° Virgo 42'
Aug 22, 1979	11:22	Solar Eclipse	29° Leo 01'
Sep 6, 1979	04:54	Lunar Eclipse	13° Pisces 15'
Feb 16, 1980	02:52	Solar Eclipse	26° Aquarius 50'
Mar 1, 1980	14:45	Lunar Eclipse	11° Virgo 26'
Jul 27, 1980	13:07	Lunar Eclipse	04° Aquarius 52'
Aug 10, 1980	13:12	Solar Eclipse	18° Leo 17'
Aug 25, 1980	21:30	Lunar Eclipse	03° Pisces 03'
Jan 20, 1981	01:50	Lunar Eclipse	00° Leo 11'
Feb 4, 1981	16:09	Solar Eclipse	16° Aquarius 01'

1980 (marginal year marker beside Feb 16, 1980 row)

Date	Time	Type	Zodiac Position
Jul 16, 1981	22:47	Lunar Eclipse	24° Capricorn 31'
Jul 30, 1981	21:45	Solar Eclipse	07° Leo 51'
Jan 9, 1982	13:56	Lunar Eclipse	19° Cancer 14'
Jan 24, 1982	22:41	Solar Eclipse	04° Aquarius 53'
Jun 21, 1982	06:03	Solar Eclipse	29° Gemini 47'
Jul 6, 1982	01:30	Lunar Eclipse	13° Capricorn 55'
Jul 20, 1982	12:44	Solar Eclipse	27° Cancer 43'
Dec 15, 1982	03:31	Solar Eclipse	23° Sagittarius 05'
Dec 30, 1982	05:28	Lunar Eclipse	08° Cancer 26'
Jun 10, 1983	22:42	Solar Eclipse	19° Gemini 43'
Jun 25, 1983	02:22	Lunar Eclipse	03° Capricorn 14'
Dec 4, 1983	06:30	Solar Eclipse	11° Sagittarius 47'
Dec 19, 1983	19:49	Lunar Eclipse	27° Gemini 36'
May 14, 1984	22:40	Lunar Eclipse	24° Scorpio 32'
May 30, 1984	10:44	Solar Eclipse	09° Gemini 26'
Jun 13, 1984	08:26	Lunar Eclipse	22° Sagittarius 44'
Nov 8, 1984	11:54	Lunar Eclipse	16° Taurus 31'
Nov 22, 1984	16:52	Solar Eclipse	00° Sagittarius 50'
May 4, 1985	13:55	Lunar Eclipse	14° Scorpio 17'
May 19, 1985	15:29	Solar Eclipse	28° Taurus 50'
Oct 28, 1985	11:41	Lunar Eclipse	05° Taurus 15'
Nov 12, 1985	08:10	Solar Eclipse	20° Scorpio 08'
Apr 9, 1986	00:20	Solar Eclipse	19° Aries 07'
Apr 24, 1986	06:43	Lunar Eclipse	04° Scorpio 03'
Oct 3, 1986	13:04	Solar Eclipse	10° Libra 16'
Oct 17, 1986	13:18	Lunar Eclipse	24° Aries 07'
Mar 29, 1987	06:48	Solar Eclipse	08° Aries 18'
Apr 13, 1987	20:19	Lunar Eclipse	23° Libra 37'

Date	Time	Type	Zodiac Position
Sep 22, 1987	21:11	Solar Eclipse	29° Virgo 34'
Oct 6, 1987	22:01	Lunar Eclipse	13° Aries 21'
Mar 3, 1988	10:13	Lunar Eclipse	13° Virgo 18'
Mar 17, 1988	19:57	Solar Eclipse	27° Pisces 42'
Aug 27, 1988	05:04	Lunar Eclipse	04° Pisces 23'
Sep 10, 1988	22:43	Solar Eclipse	18° Virgo 40'
Feb 20, 1989	09:34	Lunar Eclipse	01° Virgo 59'
Mar 7, 1989	12:08	Solar Eclipse	17° Pisces 09'
Aug 16, 1989	21:08	Lunar Eclipse	24° Aquarius 12'
Aug 30, 1989	23:30	Solar Eclipse	07° Virgo 48'
Jan 26, 1990	13:30	Solar Eclipse	06° Aquarius 35'
Feb 9, 1990	13:11	Lunar Eclipse	20° Leo 47'
Jul 21, 1990	21:01	Solar Eclipse	29° Cancer 04'
Aug 6, 1990	08:12	Lunar Eclipse	13° Aquarius 52'
Jan 15, 1991	17:53	Solar Eclipse	25° Capricorn 20'
Jan 29, 1991	23:59	Lunar Eclipse	09° Leo 50'
Jun 26, 1991	21:14	Lunar Eclipse	05° Capricorn 00'
Jul 11, 1991	13:06	Solar Eclipse	18° Cancer 59'
Jul 26, 1991	12:08	Lunar Eclipse	03° Aquarius 16'
Dec 21, 1991	04:32	Lunar Eclipse	29° Gemini 03'
Jan 4, 1992	17:04	Solar Eclipse	13° Capricorn 51'
Jun 14, 1992	22:57	Lunar Eclipse	24° Sagittarius 21'
Jun 30, 1992	06:10	Solar Eclipse	08° Cancer 56'
Dec 9, 1992	17:43	Lunar Eclipse	18° Gemini 10'
Dec 23, 1992	18:31	Solar Eclipse	02° Capricorn 27'
May 21, 1993	08:18	Solar Eclipse	00° Gemini 32'
Jun 4, 1993	06:59	Lunar Eclipse	13° Sagittarius 55'

1990

Date	Time	Type	Zodiac Position
Nov 13, 1993	15:45	Solar Eclipse	21° Scorpio 32'
Nov 29, 1993	00:25	Lunar Eclipse	07° Gemini 03'
May 10, 1994	11:10	Solar Eclipse	19° Taurus 49'
May 24, 1994	21:30	Lunar Eclipse	03° Sagittarius 43'
Nov 3, 1994	07:38	Solar Eclipse	10° Scorpio 54'
Nov 18, 1994	00:44	Lunar Eclipse	25° Taurus 42'
Apr 15, 1995	06:17	Lunar Eclipse	25° Libra 04'
Apr 29, 1995	11:32	Solar Eclipse	08° Taurus 56'
Oct 8, 1995	10:03	Lunar Eclipse	14° Aries 54'
Oct 23, 1995	22:31	Solar Eclipse	00° Scorpio 17'
Apr 3, 1996	18:09	Lunar Eclipse	14° Libra 31'
Apr 17, 1996	16:37	Solar Eclipse	28° Aries 11'
Sep 26, 1996	20:53	Lunar Eclipse	04° Aries 17'
Oct 12, 1996	08:02	Solar Eclipse	19° Libra 31'
Mar 8, 1997	19:24	Solar Eclipse	18° Pisces 31'
Mar 23, 1997	22:39	Lunar Eclipse	03° Libra 35'
Sep 1, 1997	18:04	Solar Eclipse	09° Virgo 34'
Sep 16, 1997	12:46	Lunar Eclipse	23° Pisces 56'
Feb 26, 1998	11:27	Solar Eclipse	07° Pisces 55'
Mar 12, 1998	22:19	Lunar Eclipse	22° Virgo 23'
Aug 7, 1998	20:25	Lunar Eclipse	15° Aquarius 22'
Aug 21, 1998	20:05	Solar Eclipse	28° Leo 48'
Sep 6, 1998	05:09	Lunar Eclipse	13° Pisces 40'
Jan 31, 1999	10:17	Lunar Eclipse	11° Leo 20'
Feb 16, 1999	00:33	Solar Eclipse	27° Aquarius 08'
Jul 28, 1999	05:34	Lunar Eclipse	04° Aquarius 58'
Aug 11, 1999	05:03	Solar Eclipse	18° Leo 21'

	Date	Time	Type	Zodiac Position
2000	Jan 20, 2000	22:42	Lunar Eclipse	00° Leo 26'
	Feb 5, 2000	06:48	Solar Eclipse	16° Aquarius 01'
	Jul 1, 2000	13:32	Solar Eclipse	10° Cancer 15'
	Jul 16, 2000	07:55	Lunar Eclipse	24° Capricorn 19'
	Jul 30, 2000	20:13	Solar Eclipse	08° Leo 11'
	Dec 25, 2000	11:35	Solar Eclipse	04° Capricorn 15'
	Jan 9, 2001	14:20	Lunar Eclipse	19° Cancer 39'
	Jun 21, 2001	06:03	Solar Eclipse	00° Cancer 11'
	Jul 5, 2001	08:54	Lunar Eclipse	13° Capricorn 39'
	Dec 14, 2001	14:52	Solar Eclipse	22° Sagittarius 56'
	Dec 30, 2001	04:29	Lunar Eclipse	08° Cancer 47'
	May 26, 2002	06:02	Lunar Eclipse	05° Sagittarius 04'
	Jun 10, 2002	17:43	Solar Eclipse	19° Gemini 54'
	Jun 24, 2002	15:26	Lunar Eclipse	03° Capricorn 11'
	Nov 19, 2002	19:45	Lunar Eclipse	27° Taurus 33'
	Dec 4, 2002	01:30	Solar Eclipse	11° Sagittarius 58'
	May 15, 2003	21:39	Lunar Eclipse	24° Scorpio 53'
	May 30, 2003	22:07	Solar Eclipse	09° Gemini 19'
	Nov 8, 2003	19:18	Lunar Eclipse	16° Taurus 13'
	Nov 23, 2003	16:49	Solar Eclipse	01° Sagittarius 14'
	Apr 19, 2004	07:33	Solar Eclipse	29° Aries 50'
	May 4, 2004	14:29	Lunar Eclipse	14° Scorpio 42'
	Oct 13, 2004	20:59	Solar Eclipse	21° Libra 06'
	Oct 27, 2004	21:03	Lunar Eclipse	05° Taurus 02'
	Apr 8, 2005	14:36	Solar Eclipse	19° Aries 06'
	Apr 24, 2005	03:55	Lunar Eclipse	04° Scorpio 19'
	Oct 3, 2005	04:31	Solar Eclipse	10° Libra 19'
	Oct 17, 2005	06:02	Lunar Eclipse	24° Aries 13'

Date	Time	Type	Zodiac Position
Mar 14, 2006	17:47	Lunar Eclipse	24° Virgo 15'
Mar 29, 2006	04:10	Solar Eclipse	08° Aries 35'
Sep 7, 2006	12:50	Lunar Eclipse	15° Pisces 00'
Sep 22, 2006	05:39	Solar Eclipse	29° Virgo 20'
Mar 3, 2007	17:20	Lunar Eclipse	13° Virgo 00'
Mar 18, 2007	20:32	Solar Eclipse	28° Pisces 07'
Aug 28, 2007	04:37	Lunar Eclipse	04° Pisces 46'
Sep 11, 2007	06:31	Solar Eclipse	18° Virgo 24'
Feb 6, 2008	21:55	Solar Eclipse	17° Aquarius 45'
Feb 20, 2008	21:25	Lunar Eclipse	01° Virgo 52'
Aug 1, 2008	04:20	Solar Eclipse	09° Leo 32'
Aug 16, 2008	15:10	Lunar Eclipse	24° Aquarius 21'
Jan 26, 2009	01:59	Solar Eclipse	06° Aquarius 30'
Feb 9, 2009	08:37	Lunar Eclipse	20° Leo 59'
Jul 7, 2009	03:38	Lunar Eclipse	15° Capricorn 25'
Jul 21, 2009	20:35	Solar Eclipse	29° Cancer 27'
Aug 5, 2009	18:39	Lunar Eclipse	13° Aquarius 43'
Dec 31, 2009	13:21	Lunar Eclipse	10° Cancer 15'
2010 Jan 15, 2010	08:05	Solar Eclipse	25° Capricorn 01'
Jun 26, 2010	12:37	Lunar Eclipse	04° Capricorn 47'
Jul 11, 2010	20:32	Solar Eclipse	19° Cancer 24'
Dec 21, 2010	09:17	Lunar Eclipse	29° Gemini 21'

---

1. Eclipse data generated by Solar Fire version 5.0.26 © Esoteric Technologies 1994–2001.

Appendix 2
How to Use the CD-ROM

First, you need to install the program. Just remove the CD-ROM from its folder, and place it in your computer's CD-ROM drive. The program will begin to install itself.

If it does not start automatically, click on the Start menu and select "Run." In the Run menu dialog box, type in your corresponding CD-ROM drive followed by the file name SETUP.exe. Typically, the CD-ROM is set up as D:\. The install wizard will run and guide you through the rest of the process.

For an alternate method, you can access your CD-ROM drive by clicking on "My Computer" and then clicking on the CD-ROM drive (typically D:\). Double-click on the SETUP.exe icon.

When you double-click on the program icon, you will see a screen called *Mapping Your Soul's Purpose*, which is pictured on the following page.

Mapping Your Soul's Purpose is a basic astrology program, designed around the most sophisticated astrology programming available. Cosmic Patterns, in collaboration with Llewellyn Worldwide, has developed this program to provide you with birth charts (the circle with all the astrological symbols) and interpretations of those charts (eight- to ten-page printouts of information about your karma and destiny).

Let's discuss the choices you have on this screen:

- The Start menu is used to create a chart.
- The About menu provides information about Llewellyn Worldwide, the publisher of *Mapping Your Soul's Purpose,* and Cosmic Patterns Software, the designer of the program.
- The Quit menu allows you to exit from the program.

Creating an Astrology Chart and Karmic Interpretation

To use your program, click on the Start menu at the top of the screen and select "New List of Charts (New Session)." If you are returning to the program and want to see the last chart you made, select "Continue with Charts of Previous Session."

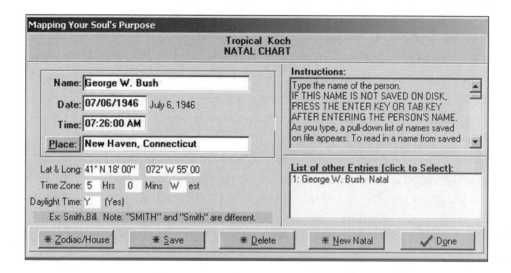

This is where you enter your birth information. There are some simple instructions on the right side of the screen, similar to what follows here. Let's make a birth chart for George W. Bush as an example. He was born on July 6, 1946, at 7:26 a.m. in New Haven, Connecticut.

- In the Name box, type "George W. Bush," and Enter.

- In the Date box, type "07061946", and Enter. (Always enter the date in mm dd yyyy format.)

- In the Time field, type "072600 AM" (the birth time in hh mm ss format), and Enter.

- In the Place box, type "New Haven, Connecticut" (the birth place). As soon as you type the word "New," a list drops down. You can continue typing, or look for New Haven, Connecticut in this list by clicking repeatedly on the down arrow.

You can go back up by clicking on the up arrow. You will see some places you have probably never heard of, but you will come to New Haven, Connecticut. Select it. The drop-down list will disappear, and you will see New Haven, Connecticut in the Place box. You will also see information filled in the boxes below it: the latitude is 41N18 00, the longitude is 072W55 00, the time zone is 5 hours 0 minutes West, and the Daylight Saving Time box is marked "Y."

If your city does not automatically come up in the list, you can use a nearby city from the list. You can also look up your birth place in an atlas to find the latitude and longitude, time zone, and daylight saving time information, and fill in this information. Generally, a city close to the birth place is close enough for most purposes and will also be in the same time zone. If the time zone information is different, your chart could be off by an hour one way or the other. Depending on the distance your choice is from your actual birth place, your chart will be slightly different. You can obtain the correct longitude, latitude, and time information from a timetable book for astrology.[1]

The Zodiac/House button allows you to select a different house system. This program automatically selects the tropical zodiac and Koch house system. Experiment with the other choices to see what changes on the chart wheel. In this program the interpretation will change only if you select the sidereal zodiac.

Select the "Save" button at the bottom of the screen to save the chart (you can delete it later if you need to), and then click "OK."

Then select the "Done" button. If you forget to save and go directly to the Done button, you will get a prompt asking if you want to save the data. In fact, all the way along prompts appear to help you enter the data.

The screen pictured on the next page is what you will see next.

---

1. Here are two possibilities: *The American Atlas*, compiled and programmed by Neil F. Michelsen (San Diego, CA: ACS Publications, 1978); and *The International Atlas*, compiled and programmed by Thomas G. Shanks (San Diego, CA: ACS Publications, 1985).

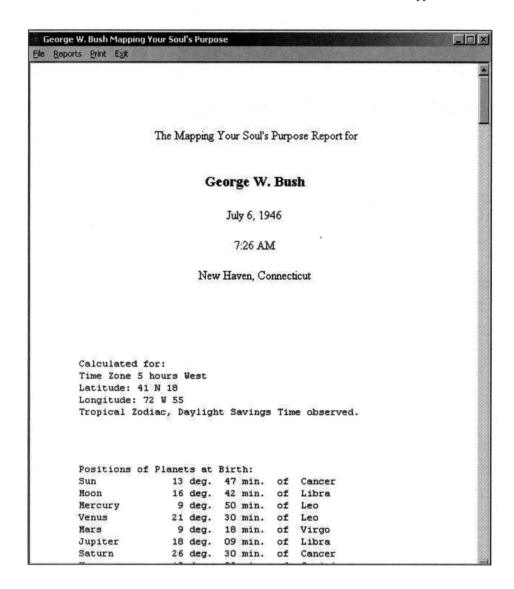

You will see George W. Bush's name and birth data, plus more information lists, and finally the interpretation. To print this interpretation, click on the Print menu and select "Print."

If you select "Wheel" from the Reports menu, a chart form appears. At the upper left corner it is labeled "Wheel Style FAC." This form should look just like the one pictured here.

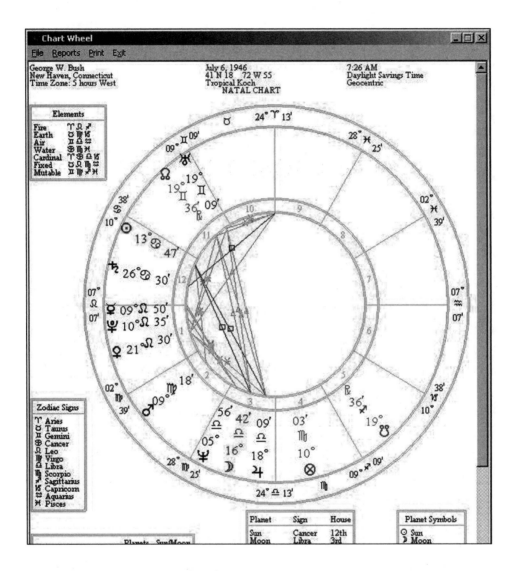

To print the chart, click on the Print menu and select "Print."

To go back to the opening screen, click on the Exit menu and select "Yes: Exit to Opening Screen." From here, you can either exit the program by clicking on the Quit menu and selecting "Yes," or you can click on the Start menu to make another chart and interpretation.

Glossary

Ascendant: The sign of the zodiac that was "rising" on the eastern horizon at the moment of birth. It clarifies what your intentions were as you started this life. It also reflects your outlook on life.

aspect: When two planets are separated by a certain number of degrees, they have a dialogue. The nature of this communication is defined by the character of the aspect. Planets do not have to be the exact number of degrees apart to be considered "in aspect." There is an orb of influence that indicates the variance allowed between two planets.

Aspect	Glyph	Meaning	Number of degrees	Orb
Conjunction	☌	Emphasis, combination	0° apart	4°
Opposition	☍	Awareness	180° apart	4°
Trine	△	Ease, harmony	120° apart	4°
Sextile	✶	Opportunity	60° apart	2°
Square	☐	Conflict, challenge	90° apart	4°
Quincunx	⚻	Adjustment	150° apart	2°

astrology: The study of the correlation between planetary phenomena and life on Earth.

astronomy: The study of planetary phenomena.

birth chart: See *chart*.

birth information: The information necessary to erect an accurate chart: (1) the birth date, (2) the exact time of birth (as noted on the birth certificate, if available), and, (3) the city, county, or district, state, and nation of birth.

chart: A map of the positions of the Sun, Moon, and planets in the zodiac at the precise moment of birth, as seen from the birth location. A chart can also include additional information, such as house divisions and aspects.

cusp: The line that separates one house from another. The sign that falls on the house cusp describes your approach to the activities of that house. Planets also affect the activities of the house in which they are positioned.

Descendant: The sign of the zodiac that was "setting" at the moment of birth. The Descendant sign makes you aware of the differences and similarities between you and the other people in your life.

Eclipse, Prenatal: Eclipses are a special alignment of the Sun, Moon, and Earth. A Solar Eclipse occurs when the Sun and Moon are in the same sign, and point to the nature of the things you have to teach others. The Lunar Eclipse occurs when the Sun and Moon are in opposite signs, and describes the lessons you intend to learn. The term *prenatal eclipse* refers to the Solar and Lunar Eclipses that occurred prior to your birth.

geocentric: This term is translated as "Earth in the center," which was based on the observations of ancient astronomers and astrologers that our planet was the center of the cosmos. Even though that theory was proven wrong hundreds of years ago in actual practice, it doesn't change Earth-centered astrology's ability to provide helpful guidance and insight.

horoscope: See *chart*.

house: The twelve chart divisions that represent different parts of life, such as health or finances. Houses are numbered, one through twelve, in a counterclockwise direction around the chart. Houses are usually an uneven division. A house is influenced by the sign on the cusp as well as any planets that are located in it.

House	Parts of Life
1	Physical body, persona
2	Money, earnings, values, self-worth
3	Education, neighborhood, siblings
4	Parents, family, home
5	Children
6	Work
7	Relationships
8	Life-changing experiences
9	Travel, religion
10	Career
11	Friends, future
12	Psychological strengths and weaknesses

IC: See *Imum Coeli.*

Imum Coeli: Latin term for nadir or low point. It describes your family heritage and your spiritual genealogy. Also referred to as the IC.

luminaries: The Sun and Moon are the brightest lights in our sky and are referred to as the lights or luminaries. The Sun and Moon are also included in the more general term *planets.*

MC: See *Medium Coeli.*

Medium Coeli: Latin term for high point or zenith. It describes your idea of success and your soul's worldly purpose.

orb: See *aspect.*

planets: The planets that orbit the Sun, plus the Sun and the Earth's Moon, are the planets that are typically included in a birth chart. The placement of each planet at the time of birth shapes the personality as follows:

Planet	Glyph	Primary Impulse
Sun	☉	To create
Moon	☽	To respond, nurture
Mercury	☿	To learn, communicate

Planet	Glyph	Primary Impulse (continued)
Venus	♀	To relate
Mars	♂	To act, fight
Jupiter	♃	To explore
Saturn	♄	To be responsible
Uranus	♅	To break with tradition
Neptune	♆	To seek out the divine
Pluto	♇	To control your fate

natal chart: See *chart*.

Prenatal Eclipse: See *Eclipse, Prenatal*.

rising sign: See *Ascendant*.

setting sign: See *Descendant*.

sign: There are twelve signs in the zodiac. They originally corresponded to the constellations with the same names, but now the signs are an equal and elegant division of the zodiac belt. Each sign reveals a distinct approach to life. Planets appear to move through the twelve signs of the zodiac at different rates, depending on their orbit around the Sun. When a planet moves through a particular sign, it expresses its own energy according to the nature of the sign, as follows:

Sign	Glyph	Manner
Aries	♈	Brave, courageous, impatient
Taurus	♉	Peaceful, stable, stubborn
Gemini	♊	Curious, young at heart, unreliable
Cancer	♋	Sensitive, emotional, moody
Leo	♌	Proud, creative, egotistical
Virgo	♍	Gentle, orderly, critical
Libra	♎	Charming, harmonious, false
Scorpio	♏	Intense, passionate, manipulative
Sagittarius	♐	Expansive, optimistic, grandiose

Sign	Glyph	Manner
Capricorn	♑	Wise, conservative, fearful
Aquarius	♒	Innovative, original, extreme
Pisces	♓	Compassionate, intuitive, escapist

zodiac: An invisible belt that extends out from the girth of the Earth, made up of twelve equal divisions called *signs*.

Bibliography

Alexander, Roy. *Meet Your Planets*. St. Paul, MN: Llewellyn Publications, 1997.

Arroyo, Stephen. *Exploring Jupiter*. Sebastopol, CA: CRCS Publications, 1996.

Avery, Jeanne. *The Rising Sign*. New York: Doubleday Publishing, 1982.

Burt, Kathleen. *Archetypes of the Zodiac*. St. Paul, MN: Llewellyn Publications, 1996.

Dobyns, Zipporah, Ph.D. *The Book of Saturn*. San Diego, CA: ACS Publications, 1996.

Forrest, Steven. *The Inner Sky*. San Diego, CA: ACS Publications, 1988.

Goldstein-Jacobson, Ivy M. *In the Beginning, Astrology*. Alhambra, CA: Frank Severy Publishing, 1975.

Greene, Liz. *The Astrology of Fate*. York Beach, ME: Samuel Weiser, 1984.

Hall, Judy. *The Karmic Journey*. New York: Arkana, 1990.

Hamaker-Zondag, Karen. *Aspects and Personality*. York Beach, ME: Samuel Weiser, 1990.

Henson, Donna. *Vertex: The Third Angle*. Tempe, AZ: American Federation of Astrologers, 2002.

Leo, Alan. *Esoteric Astrology*. 1913. Reprint, New York: Astrologer's Library, 1978.

Lineman, Rose. *Your Prenatal Eclipse*. Tempe, AZ: American Federation of Astrologers, 1992.

Pottenger, Maritha. *The East Point and the Antivertex*. San Diego, CA: Astro Communications Services, 1984.

Schulman, Martin. *Karmic Astrology: Joy and the Part of Fortune*. York Beach, ME: Samuel Weiser, 1978.

Spiller, Jan. *Astrology for the Soul*. New York: Bantam Books, 1997.

Spiller, Jan, and Karen McCoy. *Spiritual Astrology*. New York: Simon & Schuster, 1988.

Tierney, Bil. *All Around the Zodiac*. St. Paul, MN: Llewellyn Publications, 2001.

———. *Twelve Faces of Saturn*. St. Paul, MN: Llewellyn Publications, 1997.

To Write to the Author

If you wish to contact the author or would like more information about this book, please write to the author in care of Llewellyn Worldwide and we will forward your request. Both the author and publisher appreciate hearing from you and learning of your enjoyment of this book and how it has helped you. Llewellyn Worldwide cannot guarantee that every letter written to the author can be answered, but all will be forwarded. Please write to:

Anne Windsor
℅ Llewellyn Worldwide
2143 Wooddale Drive, Dept. 0-7387-0673-6
Woodbury, MN 55125-2989, U.S.A.

Please enclose a self-addressed stamped envelope for reply,
or $1.00 to cover costs. If outside U.S.A., enclose
international postal reply coupon.

Many of Llewellyn's authors have websites with additional information and resources. For more information, please visit our website at
http://www.llewellyn.com.